First World War
and Army of Occupation
War Diary
France, Belgium and Germany

3 DIVISION
8 Infantry Brigade
Gordon Highlanders
1st Battalion
4 August 1914 - 31 October 1915

WO95/1421/1

The Naval & Military Press Ltd
www.nmarchive.com
Published in association with The National Archives

Published by

The Naval & Military Press Ltd

Unit 10 Ridgewood Industrial Park,

Uckfield, East Sussex,

TN22 5QE England

Tel: +44 (0) 1825 749494

www.naval-military-press.com

www.nmarchive.com

This diary has been reprinted in facsimile from the original. Any imperfections are inevitably reproduced and the quality may fall short of modern type and cartographic standards.

Contents

Document type	Place/Title	Date From	Date To
War Diary	Crownhill Phymouth	04/08/1914	13/08/1914
War Diary	Plymouth	13/08/1914	13/08/1914
War Diary	Southampton	13/08/1914	13/08/1914
War Diary	Boulogne	14/08/1914	14/08/1914
War Diary	St Martin Near Boulogne	14/08/1914	15/08/1914
War Diary	Boulogne Station	16/08/1914	16/08/1914
War Diary	Aulnoye	16/08/1914	16/08/1914
War Diary	Taisnieres	16/08/1914	20/08/1914
War Diary	St Aubin	20/08/1914	21/08/1914
War Diary	1/2 Mile N Of Le Dave 2 1/2 Mile S Of Maubeuge	21/08/1914	21/08/1914
War Diary	Goegnies	21/08/1914	22/08/1914
War Diary	Audencourt	26/08/1914	27/08/1914
War Diary	S Of Clary	27/08/1914	28/08/1914
War Diary	Genvry	28/08/1914	29/08/1914
War Diary	Guts	30/08/1914	30/08/1914
War Diary	Courtieux	30/08/1914	31/08/1914
War Diary	Vaumoise	31/08/1914	01/09/1914
War Diary	Chevreville	01/09/1914	02/09/1914
War Diary	Fortry	02/09/1914	02/09/1914
War Diary	Monthyon	02/09/1914	03/09/1914
War Diary	Nanteuil	03/09/1914	03/09/1914
War Diary	S Of Boutigny	03/09/1914	04/09/1914
War Diary	Retal	05/09/1914	05/09/1914
War Diary	Les Corvelles	08/09/1914	08/09/1914
War Diary	1 Mile N of Rebais	08/09/1914	08/09/1914
War Diary	Just S of Gibraltar	08/09/1914	08/09/1914
War Diary	1/2 Mile S of Orly	08/09/1914	08/09/1914
War Diary	Fer-En-Tardenois	20/09/1914	30/09/1914
War Diary	Courcelles	01/10/1914	01/10/1914
War Diary	Oulchy	02/10/1914	02/10/1914
Miscellaneous	8th Infty Bde 1st Bn Gordon Highlanders		
Heading	8th Brigade 1st Gordon Highlanders Vol III 1-30.11.14		
War Diary	Croix-De-Poperinghe	01/11/1914	07/11/1914
War Diary	In Trenches Near Hooge E of Ypres	07/11/1914	11/11/1914
War Diary	Westoutre	21/11/1914	25/11/1914
War Diary	Locre	26/11/1914	29/11/1914
War Diary	In Trenches Near Kemmel on Right of The Kemmel-Wytschaete Road	29/11/1914	30/11/1914
War Diary	In Billets in Locre	04/12/1914	12/12/1914
War Diary	Kemmel	13/12/1914	18/12/1914
War Diary	In Trenches E of Kemmel	19/12/1914	20/12/1914
War Diary	In Billets At Westoutre	21/12/1914	04/01/1915
War Diary	In Billets In La Clytte	05/01/1915	08/01/1915
War Diary	In Trenches Near Vierstraat	09/01/1915	20/01/1915
War Diary	In Billets In La Clytte	21/01/1915	24/01/1915
War Diary	In Trenches Near Vierstraat	25/01/1915	28/01/1915
War Diary	In Billets at La Clytte	01/02/1915	01/02/1915
War Diary	In Trenches Near Vierstraat	02/02/1915	05/02/1915
War Diary	In Billets In La Clytte	06/02/1915	09/02/1915
War Diary	In Trenches Near Vierstraat	10/02/1915	13/02/1915

War Diary	In Billets In La Clytte	14/02/1915	16/02/1915
War Diary	In Trenches Near Vierstraat	17/02/1915	19/02/1915
War Diary	In Billets In La Clytte	22/02/1915	23/02/1915
War Diary	In Trenches Near Vierstraat	24/02/1915	26/02/1915
War Diary	La Clytte	01/03/1915	04/03/1915
War Diary	Trenches Near Vierstraat (Section K2&L)	05/03/1915	05/03/1915
War Diary	Trenches Near Vierstraat	06/03/1915	08/03/1915
War Diary	In Billets at La Clytte	09/03/1915	12/03/1915
War Diary	In Trenches (N) North of Vierstraat	01/04/1915	30/04/1915
Miscellaneous	1 Gordon April 1915		
Map	Map		
Miscellaneous	1 Gordon April 1915		
War Diary	Hooge	28/05/1915	08/06/1915
War Diary	In Bivouac	09/06/1915	09/06/1915
War Diary	In Bivouac At Brandhoek	10/06/1915	13/06/1915
War Diary	Ypres	15/06/1915	18/06/1915
War Diary	Brandhoek	23/06/1915	17/07/1915
War Diary	Hooge Trenches	20/07/1915	22/07/1915
War Diary	Brandhoek Bivouac	23/07/1915	23/07/1915
War Diary	Brandhoek	24/07/1915	24/07/1915
War Diary	Trenches Near Verbrandenmolen	25/07/1915	26/07/1915
War Diary	Trenches	26/07/1915	28/07/1915
War Diary	Verbrandenmolen	29/07/1915	29/07/1915
War Diary	Trenches	29/07/1915	30/07/1915
War Diary	Verbrandenmolen Trenches	31/07/1915	31/07/1915
Map	Map		
War Diary		04/08/1915	04/08/1915
War Diary	Same Bivouac	05/08/1915	22/08/1915
War Diary	Same Trenches	23/08/1915	23/08/1915
War Diary	Bivouac Near Ouderdom	24/08/1915	27/08/1915
War Diary	Same Bivouac	28/08/1915	28/08/1915
War Diary	Bivouac at Farm H19c.0.3	01/09/1915	01/09/1915
War Diary	Bivouac at Farm H 13. D.5.5	02/09/1915	03/09/1915
War Diary	Same Bivouac	06/09/1915	11/09/1915
War Diary	Hooge Trenches 1.18.B	12/09/1915	14/09/1915
War Diary	Bivouac Farm H.13.D.5.5	19/09/1915	28/09/1915
War Diary	Trenches 1.24 Bv D	29/09/1915	30/09/1915
Map	Map		
Miscellaneous	1st Bn Gordon Highlanders	25/09/1915	25/09/1915
War Diary	Trenches 124. B & D	11/10/1915	15/10/1915
War Diary	Barus And Dugouts H 23 B	21/10/1915	22/10/1915
War Diary	Billets at Eecke	23/10/1915	31/10/1915

Instructions regarding War Diaries and Intelligence Summaries are contained in F. S. Regs., Part II. and the Staff Manual respectively. Title pages will be prepared in manuscript.

August 1914

WAR DIARY
or
INTELLIGENCE SUMMARY.
(Erase heading not required.)

Army Form C. 2118.

1st Gordon Highlanders.

Hour, Date, Place	Summary of Events and Information	Remarks and references to Appendices
1914		
5.20 pm 4th Aug. Crownhill Plymouth	Order to mobilize received by telephone and acknowledged.	
5th " "	Mobilization Equipment drawn and SAA ammunition drawn from GUNWHARF and BULL POINT respectively:	
6.0 pm 6th " "	236 Reservists arrived from the Depot ABERDEEN.	
11.55 pm 7th " "	296 Reservists arrived from " " "	
4.0 pm 8th " "	Mobilisation complete less 2 Captains	
10.0 am 10th " "	Battalion inspected by B.G.C. 8th Infantry Brigade	
3.30 pm " "	Battalion completed to War Strength	
11.0 pm 11th " "	15 Reservists arrived from the Depot. ABERDEEN.	
12. noon 12th " "	Orders issued to Battalion to entrain	
12. midnight " "	1st train party under Lt Col F. H. Neish marched off from CROWNHILL HUTMENTS	
1.45 am 13th "	2nd Train - - Bt Col W. E. Gordon V.C. ADC " "	
2.30 " PLYMOUTH	1st train - left FRIARY STN (LSWR) PLYMOUTH	
4.21 " "	2nd - - "	
9.30 " SOUTHAMPTON	1st - - arrived at SOUTHAMPTON and embarked on the Hired Transport "ABINSI"	
11.40 " "	2nd - - "	
2.45 pm " "	"ABINSI" with Battalion on board (less 2Lt H.L.P. Burn with 11 NCOs and men in charge of 11 horses on board the SS "MOMBASSA") left SOUTHAMPTON DOCKS.	
4.15 AM 14th BOULOGNE	arrived at BOULOGNE and disembarked.	
" ST MARTIN near BOULOGNE	Battalion in rest camp at St MARTIN on the outskirts of BOULOGNE. Strength of Battalion 28 Officers, 1 Warrant Officer 987 other ranks. See appendix I	APPENDIX I attached Roll of Officers taking the field

Instructions regarding War Diaries and Intelligence Summaries are contained in F. S. Regs., Part II. and the Staff Manual respectively. Title pages will be prepared in manuscript.

WAR DIARY
or
INTELLIGENCE SUMMARY.
(Erase heading not required.)

Army Form C. 2118.

1st Gordon Highlanders.

Hour, Date, Place 1914	Summary of Events and Information	Remarks and references to Appendices
11 am 15th August. St Martin BOULOGNE	Battalion paraded and was inspected by the French G.O.C Lines of Communications afterwards went for a short route march.	
10·40 pm " "	Battalion paraded and marched to BOULOGNE STATION where it entrained. The whole entrainment including horses and transport wagons was completed in 1½ hours.	
3·55 AM 16th – BOULOGNE STATION	Train left BOULOGNE	
~~2·10~~ 2·30 PM " AULNOYE	Arrived at AULNOYE Battalion detrained and marched about ¼ mile to a field where they remained till 5·40 pm and had dinners.	
5·40 pm – "	Left AULNOYE and marched to TAISNIERES about 4 miles away where the Battn went into Billets	
7·0 pm – – TAISNIERES	Battalion arrived and went into Billets* See Appendix 2	* See Appendix II attached
17th August "	Battalion went for route marches by companies in the Brigade Area	
18th – "		
19th – "	Orders received to move on the following day to ST AUBIN	
8·50 am 20th	Battalion left TAISNIERES at 8·50 am and marched via DOMPIERE to ST AUBIN	
11·0 am 20th – ST AUBIN	Battalion arrived 11 am after a very hot march and went into Billets*	* See Appendix III attached
10·45 pm " –	Orders received for the Battalion to move at 6·15 am following day in direction of MAUBERGE destination unknown	
1·40 am 21st "	Fresh orders received from Bde ordering Battalion together with 2/R Scots 2 troops cavalry to form an advanced guard to the Right column of the 3rd Division moving along main AVESNES – MAUBERGE road and to start at 5·10 am. Col W.E. Gordon VC ADC was appointed advance guard commander	
87·30 am 21st – ½ mile N of LE PAVÉ 2½ miles S of MAUBEUGE	Battalion as part of main guard ~~[illegible]~~ halted for 1 hour owing to Cavalry Division crossing main road to the EAST.	
10·40 am –	Battalion passed through MAUBEUGE which was being	
3·15 pm – GOEGNIES	Battalion arrived and went into Billets some in French and some in Belgian Territory found a platoon as guard over Divisional Head Quarters, also examining posts on two roads in Battn Area. The Battalion though only marching about 15 miles had a long and tiring day	
3 am 22nd "	Orders received for Battalion to ~~move at 5·~~ pass starting point at 8·45 am	
4·55 am – –	Fresh orders received for previous time to be advanced by 1½ hours.	

(9 26 6) W 257—976 100,000 4/12 H W V 79/3298

Instructions regarding War Diaries and Intelligence Summaries are contained in F. S. Regs., Part II. and the Staff Manual respectively. Title pages will be prepared in manuscript.

WAR DIARY
or
INTELLIGENCE SUMMARY.
(Erase heading not required.)

Army Form C. 2118.

1st Gordon Highlanders.

Hour, Date, Place	Summary of Events and Information	Remarks and references to Appendices
4.30 pm 26-8-14 AUDENCOURT.	Order to retire does not appear to have reached Bn H-Q & remaining Coys -	
12 m.n. 26/27-8-14 "	Bn H-Q & 3 Coys less platoon commenced retirement -	
2 am. 27-8-14 S. of CLARY -	3 Coys less platoon Battalion engaged - with enemy - while endeavouring to fall back and join Brigade -	
6 pm 27-8-14	Part of Battalion joined Brigade - Officers now present with the Battalion Capts Marshall & Fowke, Lieut Sandeman 2nd Lt Turnbull Lt & 2' Mr MacDonald - and 215 other ranks -	
Night of 27/28th	Marched all night : arrived at HAM 4 am	
28th Aug 6-30 pm GENVRY	Bivouaced for the night	
2 pm 29th Aug GENVRY	Commenced march to GUTS	
1 am 30th " GUTS	Bivouaced for 4 hours	
5.30 am -	marched to COURTIEUX	
6 pm " COURTIEUX	went into bivouac.	
7 am 31st " COURTIEUX	marched to VAVMOISE	
6 pm " VAVMOISE	went into bivouac: with outlying picquet of 1 Coy as reserve for outposts	

Sept 1914

Instructions regarding War Diaries and Intelligence Summaries are contained in F. S. Regs., Part II. and the Staff Manual respectively. Title pages will be prepared in manuscript.

WAR DIARY
or
INTELLIGENCE SUMMARY.
(Erase heading not required.)

Army Form C. 2118.

1st Gordon Highlanders.

Hour, Date, Place		Summary of Events and Information	Remarks and references to Appendices
7 am. 1st Sept.	VAUMOISE	Marched to CHEVREVILLE	
6 pm — —	CHEVREVILLE	went into billets.	
2 am. 2nd Sept. 14	CHEVREVILLE	Battalion moved off as escort to divisional ammunition column at BREGY.	
8 am — —	FORTRY.	Battalion rejoined Brigade.	
2 pm. — —	MONTHYON.	Battalion went into billets. furnishing a picquet at the S.W entrance of the Village.	
7 am. 3rd — —	MONTHYON	Battalion moved to take up a position East of the FORET de MANS to be held by the 3rd Division in conjunction with the remainder of the army. route via PENCHARD — MEAUX — BOUTIGNY.	
4 pm. — —	NANTEUIL ~~BOUTIGNY~~	On arrival at NANTEUIL-LES-MEAUX the battalion was ordered to hold a section of the outpost line from P. in [illegible] x roads just N-W of P in LE PT ST LOUP to X roads W. of P in PREVILLIERS. both inclusive. The Brigade went into billets at VAUCOURTOIS.	
5 pm — — —	S. of BOUTIGNY.	Battalion entrenched outpost position.	
3.30 am. 4th Sept.	— —	Outposts stood to arms. and occupied outpost position during the day.	
1. pm.	— — —	German cavalry patrols reported in NANTEUIL	
2.5 pm — —	— — —	Order received from Bde H.Q. for outposts to be ready to retire to SANCY at short notice.	
5 pm. — —	— — —	Battalion ordered to retire through SANCHY to LA CHAPRELLE and there await orders: rejoined remainder of Brigade just S. of VAUCOURTOIS;	
8 am. 5th Sept.	RETAL.	Marched all night and went into billets at 8 am at RETAL.	

(— 08 6) W 257—976 100,000 1/12 H W V 79/3298

Instructions regarding War Diaries and Intelligence Summaries are contained in F. S. Regs., Part II. and the Staff Manual respectively. Title pages will be prepared in manuscript.

WAR DIARY
or
INTELLIGENCE SUMMARY.
(Erase heading not required.)

1st Gordon Highlanders.

Army Form C. 2118.

Hour, Date, Place	Summary of Events and Information	Remarks and references to Appendices
5 am - 8th Sept - 1914 LES CORVELLES.	The 8th Brigade Group furnished the ~~acted as~~ Advanced Guard to the 3rd Division. The 1/Gordon Highlanders and Royal Irish Regiment with 1 Battery 40th Brigade R.F.A and 1 section Composite Fd. Coy R.E formed the Advanced Guard - under Major Daniell - Royal Irish Regt. The A G moved at 5 am via St DENIS-LE-REBAIS — REBAIS towards the village of ORLY.	
7 am - - - - 1 mile N. of REBAIS.	The protective cavalry about this time was held up near the village of ~~St~~ GIBRALTAR by the enemys shell fire. The Advanced Infantry was ordered to move up through the cavalry which had halted in the woods just North of the village of GIBRALTAR. The Royal Irish Regiment extended into lines of small columns on the East side of the main road and the 1st Gordon Highlanders advanced in a similar formation on the west side of the main road	

Instructions regarding War Diaries and Intelligence Summaries are contained in F. S. Regs., Part II. and the Staff Manual respectively. Title pages will be prepared in manuscript.

WAR DIARY
or
INTELLIGENCE SUMMARY.
(Erase heading not required.)

1st Gordon Highlanders -

Army Form C. 2118.

Hour, Date, Place	Summary of Events and Information	Remarks and references to Appendices
8-40 am - 8th Sept - 1914 just S. of GIBRALTAR	On passing the village the enemy opened with shrapnel on the advanced guard infantry - owing to the extended formations little damage was done - The Battalion advanced in two lines; the first No1. Company under Capt TOWKE and the second No 2 Company under Lt HUME-GORE The position of the Comg Officer was with the 1st line - Owing to the extreme thickness of the woods in the valley of the PETIT MORIN slow progress was made -	
10 am. 8th Sept. 1914 ½ mile S. of ORLY	On reaching the bend of the road N. of the L in LE MONCEL the enemy were seen on the N- side of the valley entrenching the line ORLY-BUSSEROLLES and shortly afterwards the battalion came under machine gun fire as well as shrapnel - The advanced guard commander now ordered the 1/Gordon Highlanders to move through the woods & engage the enemys right while the Royal Irish held them in front.	

(9 26 6) W 257—976 100,000 4/12 H W V 79/3298

Instructions regarding War Diaries and Intelligence Summaries are contained in F. S. Regs., Part II. and the Staff Manual respectively. Title pages will be prepared in manuscript.

WAR DIARY
or
INTELLIGENCE SUMMARY.
(Erase heading not required.)

Army Form C. 2118.

1st Gordon Highlanders.

Hour, Date, Place	Summary of Events and Information	Remarks and references to Appendices
4 pm 20th Sept 14 TER-EN-TARDENOIS	2Lt GRIFFEN proceeded with 20 men to the base as escort to German prisoners.	
	2 Officers and 57 other ranks.	
6 pm --	CHURCH PARADE.	
9 pm --	Lt. JOHNSTON-WATSON returned from 10th Bde with 3rd reinforcement which had been attached to 2/SEAFORTH HIGHLANDERS. (Strength of re-inforcement less Casualties with 2/Seaforth Highrs 77 NCOs & men)	
	The following letters were brought by Lt JOHNSTON-WATSON from Br. Gen A. HALDANE and Capt STOCKWELL Comdg 2 Seaforth Highlanders.	
	"O.C. 1 Gordon Highlanders.	
	I think you will be glad to hear that the reinforcements for the 1st Bn Gordon Highlanders who were attached to the 2nd Bn Seaforth Highlanders pending their joining their own Corps were sent forward to re-inforce the left of the SEAFORTH Highlanders on the 14th under Lt MURRAY. They advanced with the greatest boldness and dash under very heavy and accurate shrapnel fire. Their officer was killed but they went forward and won the admiration of the Seaforths. They are as fine a draft as I have ever seen and it is with great regret that I part with them. They are true Gordon Highlanders "Sans peur and sans reproche."	
	Bucy-le-Long 9.30 am 17-9-14 Sd A. Haldane. Br. General. Comdg 10th Inf Bde.	
	1/Gn Hrs Losses already reported on 14th Killed 1 Officer, wounded other ranks 18.	

Instructions regarding War Diaries and Intelligence Summaries are contained in F.S. Regs., Part II. and the Staff Manual respectively. Title pages will be prepared in manuscript.

WAR DIARY
or
INTELLIGENCE SUMMARY.
(Erase heading not required.)

Army Form C. 2118.

1st Gordon Highlanders.

Hour, Date, Place	Summary of Events and Information	Remarks and references to Appendices
9 pm 20 Sept. in FER-EN-TARDENOIS	19-9-14 - O.C. 1/Gordon Highlanders I have the greatest pleasure in reporting to you that the detachment of your battalion which has been with us since the 8th and is now returning, has been a credit to your Regiment. They have endured the hardships through which we have passed with the most perfect good discipline & fortitude, and in action have displayed a coolness & courage which we have all admired. I greatly regret their casualties (including Lt MURRAY) details of which I have given to Lieut JOHNSTON-WATSON. Sd C.B. Stockwell - Capt actg O.C. 2nd Leinster Regt"	
9.30 am 21 - - -	Battalion parade Inspection of draft - letters of General HALDANE and Capt STOCKWELL read to the Battalion -	
7.30 pm - - -	2/Lieut McPHERSON + 50 men returned from base from escort duty with German prisoners	
- - -	No 8904 Pte Robert Elder Walker - recommended for the "Medaille Militaire"	

Instructions regarding War Diaries and Intelligence Summaries are contained in F. S. Regs., Part II. and the Staff Manual respectively. Title pages will be prepared in manuscript.

WAR DIARY
or
INTELLIGENCE SUMMARY.
(Erase heading not required.)

Army Form C. 2118.

1st Gordon Highlanders.

Hour, Date, Place	Summary of Events and Information	Remarks and references to Appendices
27th Sept. 1914. FER-EN-TARDENOIS.	Voluntary Church parade.	
28th -- -- } 29th -- -- -- }	Route marching entrenching and skirmishing by companies	
2-30pm 30th -- -- --	SUFFOLK Regiment took the place of the battalion as Army Troops. The Battalion marched via BRAINE to COURCELLES to rejoin 8th Brigade arriving about 7-30 pm. Lt General Sir Nevil Macready addressed the Battalion before marching off from FER-EN-TARDENOIS, and expressed his pleasure at the smartness, soldierly bearing and good conduct of the battalion during their tour of duty at General Head Quarters.	
4 pm. 1st Oct. 14 COURCELLES.	Brigade ordered to move at 7-15 pm. via AUGY, ARCY, and BÈVENEUX to OULCHY-LE-CHATEAU: reached destination 3-30 am. 2nd Oct.	
3-30 am. 2nd .. OULCHY.	Went into billets, posting picquets on the two roads leading North	

8th Infty Bde 1st Bn Gordon Highlanders

Unit.	Officers Killed	Officers Wounded	Officers Missing		Other Ranks Killed	Other Ranks Wounded	Other Ranks Missing
12. 10. 14		Capt R.B. Campbell J.J.G. MacWilliam			6	19	
[illegible] 10. 14		2/Lt A.M.B. Norman Lt H.A.F. Sandeman 2/Lt D.R. Turnbull		}	2	47	
[illegible] 10. 14	Capt A.M. Ker			}			
[illegible] 10. 14					10	25	
18. 10. 14					7	1	
21. 10. 14					3	9	2
22. 10. 14						1	
24. 10. 14	Capt L. Gordon-Duff	2/Lt D.E. Macpherson Lt J.M.J. McGrigor 2/Lt C.A.J. Graffin Lt A.D.P. Campbell	Capt J.H.A. Fowke Lt J.F. Johnson-Watson 2/Lt M.H.O. Forbes " H.A. Revill-Davies Lt A.E.A. Miller-Stirling				

19th Nov. – Good effect of direct communication between infantry trenches & artillery – Not worth sending to M.T.?

8th Brigade
7th

121
4197

1st Gordon Highlanders

Vol III 1 – 30.11.14

3298

Instructions regarding War Diaries and Intelligence Summaries are contained in F. S. Regs., Part II. and the Staff Manual respectively. Title pages will be prepared in manuscript.

1914.

or

INTELLIGENCE SUMMARY.

(*Erase heading not required.*)

1st Bn The Gordon Highlanders.

Hour, Date, Place	Summary of Events and Information	Remarks and references to Appendices
CROIX-DE-POPERINGHE 1st Nov. 1914.	Battalion arrived and went into billets. This day Brevet-Major A.W.F. Baird D.S.O. joined the Battalion and assumed command.	7 5 28
2nd - 4th Nov.	In billets at CROIX-DE-POPERINGHE.	
5th Nov.	The Battalion marched as part of the 7th Brigade to take over trenches from the 20th Brigade S. of the MENIN-YPRES road near HOOGE. Part of the line taken over was that held at this time by the 2nd Battalion of The Gordon Highlanders. In the absence of the Brigadier, who was temporarily in command of the 3rd Division, Major Baird had command of the Brigade. At this time the 7th Bde consisted of The 1st Wiltshire Regt, the 2nd S. Lancashire Regt, the 1st Royal Irish Rifles & the 1st Gordon Highlanders. The 3 latter being very much under strength. The strength of the Battalion at this time was 18 officers & 550 other ranks. The trench line occupied by the Brigade was held by 2 Battalions at a time, these being relieved every 48 hours.	
6th - 7th Nov.	Nothing of note occurred. The Germans shelled our trenches	

(9 26 6) W 257—976 100,000 4/12 H W V 79/3298

Army Form C. 2118.

WAR DIARY
or
INTELLIGENCE SUMMARY.
(Erase heading not required.)

1st Bn The Gordon Highlanders.

Instructions regarding War Diaries and Intelligence Summaries are contained in F. S. Regs., Part II. and the Staff Manual respectively. Title pages will be prepared in manuscript.

1914.

Hour, Date, Place	Summary of Events and Information	Remarks and references to Appendices
6th – 7th Nov. 1914. (Contd) In trenches. near HOOGE. E. of YPRES.	# & the ground occupied by our reserves in rear. Casualties for these 2 days amounted to 3 killed & 6 wounded.	
8th Nov. do:	Two drafts of 50 and 61 men respectively arrived in the evening under the command of Captain Duncan Campbell D.S.O. 3rd Black Watch, & Captain H.P. Burn, [recently adjutant of the 6th Bn. The Gordon Highlanders (T.F.). Three men of Captain Campbell's draft were wounded by shrapnel on the YPRES – HOOGE road on their way to join. No notice had been received of the impending arrival of these drafts, the Commanding Officer being apprised of the fact after dark on his return from the trenches.]	75
9th Nov. do:	Captain H.P. Burn took over the duties of adjutant this day.	
11th Nov. do:	The Germans attacked the trenches at dawn but were easily repulsed with the loss of 1 sergeant killed & 2 Lieut.	

Instructions regarding War Diaries and Intelligence Summaries are contained in F. S. Regs., Part II. and the Staff Manual respectively. Title pages will be prepared in manuscript.

1914.

WAR DIARY
or
INTELLIGENCE SUMMARY.
(Erase heading not required.)

1st Gordon Highlanders.

Army Form C. 2118.

Hour, Date, Place	Summary of Events and Information	Remarks and references to Appendices
WESTOUTRE. 21st – 25th 1914.	The Battalion remained in billets during this period, the time being occupied in resting, reclothing & making good losses in equipment etc.	7
LOCRE. 26th Nov. 1914.	This day the Battalion marched to LOCRE (3m.) & went into billets there.	
LOCRE. 27th – 29th Nov.	The Battalion remained in billets at LOCRE.	
In trenches near KEMMEL, on right of the KEMMEL – WYTSCHAETE road. 30th Nov.	The Battalion moved into the trenches taking over the part of the line held by the 7th Fusiliers.	

(9 26 6) W 257—976 100,000 4/12 H W V 79/3298

Instructions regarding War Diaries and Intelligence Summaries are contained in F. S. Regs., Part II. and the Staff Manual respectively. Title pages will be prepared in manuscript.

1914.

WAR DIARY
or
INTELLIGENCE SUMMARY.
(Erase heading not required.)

December. Page 2.

Army Form C. 2118.

1st Bn The Gordon Highlanders.

Hour, Date, Place	Summary of Events and Information	Remarks and references to Appendices
Dec 4th in billets in LOCRE.	Captain W. M. K. Marshall rejoined the Battalion from a months' leave home.	
	A draft of 110 N.C.O.s & men under the command of 2 Lieut R. T. Grant, 4th Argyll & Sutherland Highlanders, ~~rejoined~~ joined from home.	75
Dec 5th Do:	This day a draft of 3 officers & 93 men joined the Battalion under the command of Lieut W. F. R. Dobie. [Lieut R. Campbell 3rd Argyll & Sutherland Highlanders & 2nd Lieut G. C. Rose 3rd Seaforth Highlanders, also joined with this draft.]	13 + 66
Dec 6th – 7th Do:	Nothing of interest occurred.	
Dec 8th Do:	This day Brigadier General Bowes, Comdg 8th Infantry Brigade inspected the Battalion	

Instructions regarding War Diaries and Intelligence Summaries are contained in F. S. Regs., Part II. and the Staff Manual respectively. Title pages will be prepared in manuscript.

WAR DIARY
or
INTELLIGENCE SUMMARY.
(Erase heading not required.)

December. Page 5. Army Form C. 2118.

1914. 1st Bn The Gordon Highlanders.

Hour, Date, Place	Summary of Events and Information	Remarks and references to Appendices
Dec 12th (contd)	the rank of Coy Sergt-Major, was killed during this reconnaissance.	
Dec 13th KEMMEL.	The Battalion left billets at 6 p.m. & marched via LOCRE to KEMMEL where it arrived about 9 p.m. & went into close billets. Heavy rain fell throughout the march. At midnight orders were received for the attack to be carried out next morning.	75 cr
Dec 14th KEMMEL.	At 2.30 a.m. the Battalion left KEMMEL. "B" & "C" Coys who were to carry out the attack occupied the advanced trenches on either side of the road leading from KEMMEL to MAEDELSTRAEDE farm. "A" & "D" Coys, which formed the reserve,	

Instructions regarding War Diaries and Intelligence Summaries are contained in F. S. Regs., Part II. and the Staff Manual respectively. Title pages will be prepared in manuscript.

1914.

WAR DIARY or INTELLIGENCE SUMMARY.

(Erase heading not required.)

December. Page 6.

1st Bn The Gordon Highlanders.

Army Form C. 2118.

Hour, Date, Place	Summary of Events and Information	Remarks and references to Appendices
Dec 14th (contd)	occupied trenches about 200 yds in rear.	
7 a.m. ×	×At 7 a.m. our artillery bombardment commenced. Many of our shells fell short of the German position, some even in rear of our reserve. Owing to the inadequate means of communication this could not be reported.×	
×		
7.45 am.	At 7.45 am., in accordance with the orders received, two platoons of "B" Coy + 2 platoons of "C" Coy advanced from the fire trenches + pushed on in extended order in spite of the very heavy * rifle fire which was immediately opened on them.× The sodden nature of the ground + the fact that the men had been standing for several hours in trenches deep in mud rendered a rapid advance impossible.×	
+		
×		

(9 26 6) W 257—976 100,000 4/12 H W V 79/3298

Instructions regarding War Diaries and Intelligence Summaries are contained in F. S. Regs., Part II. and the Staff Manual respectively. Title pages will be prepared in manuscript.

1914.

WAR DIARY
or
INTELLIGENCE SUMMARY.
(Erase heading not required.)

December. Page 7.

Army Form C. 2118.

1st Bn The Gordon Highlanders.

Hour, Date, Place	Summary of Events and Information	Remarks and references to Appendices
Dec 14th (contd.)	The remaining 2 platoons of each of these coys followed their leading platoons at a distance of 50 yards.	
	"D" Coy from the reserve ~~who~~ was then brought up & sent forward in support of the left. The remaining reserve coy ("A" Coy) then occupied the whole of the line of trenches from which the attack had been launched, thus forming with a detachment of the Northumberland Fusiliers & some maxim guns, a garrison for these trenches.	
	The heavy rifle & machine gun fire which was opened from the German trenches showed at once that the artillery Bombardment had failed in its purpose & that the German trenches were still strongly held.	
	Many casualties occurred as our men left	

Instructions regarding War Diaries and Intelligence Summaries are contained in F. S. Regs., Part II. and the Staff Manual respectively. Title pages will be prepared in manuscript.

1914.

WAR DIARY
or
INTELLIGENCE SUMMARY.
(Erase heading not required.)

December. Page 8.

Army Form C. 2118.

1st Bn The Gordon Highlanders.

Hour, Date, Place	Summary of Events and Information	Remarks and references to Appendices
Dec 14th (contd)	the trenches but the advance was not checked. The attacking coys soon disappeared from view & in default of any means of communicating with them it was impossible to tell how they were progressing.	
8 a.m.	At 8 a.m, several men in our fire trenches reported that they had seen some of our men jumping down into the German trenches which were visible about 300 yards off, but the enemy were still keeping up a very hot fire on our fire trenches & on the ground immediately in front of them.	
9 a.m.	As time passed without any message coming back from the attacking lines, at 9 a.m. an attempt was made to get in touch with them by orderly, but without success.	

(9 26 6) W 257—976 100,000 4/12 H W V 79/3298

Instructions regarding War Diaries and Intelligence Summaries are contained in F.S. Regs., Part II. and the Staff Manual respectively. Title pages will be prepared in manuscript.

1914.

WAR DIARY
or
INTELLIGENCE SUMMARY.
(Erase heading not required.)

December. Page 9.

1st Bn The Gordon Highlanders.

Army Form C. 2118.

Hour, Date, Place	Summary of Events and Information	Remarks and references to Appendices
Dec 14th (contd)	Telephonic communication with Brigade H.Qrs has by now entirely failed.	
10.55 am.	An ammunition carrier who had followed the firing line returned & reported that the attacking Coys had not, when he left them, succeeded in reaching the German trenches, but that they were lying in extended order some 50 yards short of them unable to advance. A message to this effect was forwarded by orderly to Brigade H.Qs.	75
2.30 p.m.	An orderly arrived from Brigade H.Q. with instructions that the Artillery Bombardment would be renewed between 3.30 & 4.0 p.m, under cover of which a fresh effort was to be made to carry the German trenches. The message also stated that 2 Coys of the	

(9 26 6) W 257—976 100,000 4/12 H W V 79/3298

Instructions regarding War Diaries and Intelligence Summaries are contained in F. S. Regs., Part II. and the Staff Manual respectively. Title pages will be prepared in manuscript.

WAR DIARY
or
INTELLIGENCE SUMMARY.
(*Erase heading not required.*)

December - Page 10. Army Form C. 2118.

1914. 1st Bn The Gordon Highlanders.

Hour, Date, Place	Summary of Events and Information	Remarks and references to Appendices
Dec 14th (contd)	Middlesex Regt were being sent up to the support trench in rear of our fire trenches as a reserve.	
	The actual situation of the firing line was still uncertain, no communication having been received from it since the attack was launched, but a fresh effort was now made to establish communication with it by means of an orderly (Pte Hyslop), & orders were sent by him in accordance with the instructions received from Bde H.Q. regarding a fresh attempt to take the trenches being made at 4 p.m.	75
4 p.m.	By this hour no reply had been received from the firing line nor had the ½ Battn of the Middlesex Regt yet reached the support trenches. To have sent the remaining reserve coy, practically the only garrison of our fire trenches, forward under	

(9 26 6) W 257—976 100,000 4/12 H W V 79/3298

Instructions regarding War Diaries and Intelligence Summaries are contained in F. S. Regs., Part II. and the Staff Manual respectively. Title pages will be prepared in manuscript.

1914.

WAR DIARY *or* **INTELLIGENCE SUMMARY.** *(Erase heading not required.)*

December. Page 11.

Army Form C. 2118.

1st Bn The Gordon Highlanders.

Hour, Date, Place	Summary of Events and Information	Remarks and references to Appendices
Dec. 14th (contd)	these circumstances appeared highly injudicious. No consultation being possible with Bde H.Q. the Commanding Officer decided that no further attempt to take the position was practicable.	
4.15 p.m.	At this hour the orderly who had been sent forward an hour previously returned having delivered his message & bringing the first news received from the firing line during the day. It came from Lieut Hume-Gore, in command of "D" Coy, & was to the effect that he was in an isolated position with about 40 men (many of them wounded) & that the German trench about 50 yards in front of him was strongly held & protected by barbed wire entanglements. He was not in touch with anyone on his right	75

(9 26 6) W 257—976 100,000 4/12 H W V 79/3298

Instructions regarding War Diaries and Intelligence Summaries are contained in F. S. Regs., Part II. and the Staff Manual respectively. Title pages will be prepared in manuscript.

WAR DIARY
or
INTELLIGENCE SUMMARY.
(Erase heading not required.)

December - Page 13. Army Form C. 2118.

1914. 1st Bn Thelgordon Highlanders.

Hour, Date, Place	Summary of Events and Information	Remarks and references to Appendices
Dec 14th (contd)	the ground gained with a view to holding it, & both detachments were therefore withdrawn to our own trenches.	
x	x Whilst this withdrawal was being carried out, 2 Lieut Smith, who was in command of a platoon of the right coy & had been severely wounded in 2 places, came back & reported that his coy had also reached one of the German forward trenches but it had lost heavily & had found all further advance barred by rifle & machine gun fire from the German main trench in front of which ran a strong lattice-work fence, the latter forming a serious obstacle. x	75
x	This coy was also ordered to withdraw.	
	Instructions were now received from Brigade HQ,	

Instructions regarding War Diaries and Intelligence Summaries are contained in F. S. Regs., Part II. and the Staff Manual respectively. Title pages will be prepared in manuscript.

1914.

WAR DIARY
or
INTELLIGENCE SUMMARY
(Erase heading not required.)

December. Page 16.

Army Form C. 2118.

1st Battn The Gordon Highlanders.

Hour, Date, Place	Summary of Events and Information	Remarks and references to Appendices
Dec 18th (contd)	Before the Battalion marched off to the trenches it was addressed by Major-General Haldane Commanding 3rd Division, who read a letter from Sir Horace Smith-Dorrien complimenting it on the very gallant way in which the attack made on Dec 14th was carried out.	
	Weather still very bad - no casualties.	
Dec 19th in trenches E. of KEMMEL.	again much rain. 2 men killed - 1 wounded.	
Dec 20th do:	again very wet. no casualties.	
Dec 21st in billets at WESTOUTRE.	The Battalion was relieved in the trenches by the Scots Fusiliers & marched to WESTOUTRE (7 miles) where it went into billets. During the day	

1247 W 3299 200,000 (E) 8/14 J.B.C. & A. Forms/C. 2118/11.

January. Page 2.

Army Form C. 2118.

Instructions regarding War Diaries and Intelligence Summaries are contained in F. S. Regs., Part II. and the Staff Manual respectively. Title pages will be prepared in manuscript.

1915.

WAR DIARY or INTELLIGENCE SUMMARY

(Erase heading not required.)

1st Battn The Gordon Highlanders.

Hour, Date, Place	Summary of Events and Information	Remarks and references to Appendices
January 4th (continued)	during the afternoon that the 8th Bde was to take over a fresh portion of the trench line from the French on the following day.	
January 5th In billets in LA CLYTTE.	The Battalion moved to LA CLYTTE, a distance of 4 miles, where it went into billets, being held in Reserve as 2 Battalions only of the Brigade were required to hold the trenches.	
January 6th do:	Lieuts G. MacDonald and G.W.A. Alexander joined from home this day.	
January 8th do:	Captain Lewis Gordon joined the Battalion this day having resigned his appointment with the Egyptian army. As the Battalion was due to take over the trenches from the 2nd Suffolk Regiment on the following day, the usual preliminary reconnaissance was carried out after dusk by the Commanding	

1247 W 3299 200,000 (E) 8/14 J.B.C. & A. Forms/C. 2118/11.

January. Page 3.
Army Form C. 2118.

WAR DIARY
or
INTELLIGENCE SUMMARY

(*Erase heading not required.*)

1st Batt The Gordon Highlanders.

Instructions regarding War Diaries and Intelligence Summaries are contained in F. S. Regs., Part II. and the Staff Manual respectively. Title pages will be prepared in manuscript.

1915.

Hour, Date, Place	Summary of Events and Information	Remarks and references to Appendices
January 8th (continued)	officer, adjutant and Company Commanders.	
January 9th In trenches near VIERSTRAAT.	Trenches on right of VIERSTRAAT-WYTSCHAETE road taken over from 2nd Suffolk Regiment. A miserably wet cold day. The trenches were quite untenable and in a hopeless state of dilapidation. The 2nd Suffolks had to some extent improved them, but having only taken them over 4 days previously from the French, there has been little time to do much.	
January 10th do:	"B" + "C" coys in the trenches. "A" + "D" in reserve in farm buildings. During the day the enemy shelled us intermittently. Casualty. Machine-gun Sergeant Andrews killed by a sniper. day fine. very wet at night.	

1247 W 3299 200,000 (E) 8/14 J.B.C. & A. Forms/C. 2118/11.

January. Page 4.

Army Form C. 2118.

WAR DIARY
or
INTELLIGENCE SUMMARY
1st Battn The Gordon Highlanders.

(Erase heading not required.)

Instructions regarding War Diaries and Intelligence Summaries are contained in F. S. Regs., Part II. and the Staff Manual respectively. Title pages will be prepared in manuscript.

1915.

Hour, Date, Place	Summary of Events and Information	Remarks and references to Appendices
January 11th in trenches near VIERSTRAAT.	2 Lieut. W. L. Gordon, 3rd Battn Seaforth Highlanders (attached) was wounded by a shrapnel bullet which came through the roof of the farm in which his Company was billeted. After dark "A" + "D" Coys relieved "B" + "C" Coys in the fire trenches. Relief carried out without casualty. Two men were wounded during the night by rifle fire. Repair + improvement of trenches carried out as usual after dark. day fine.	
January 12th Do:	Much work done in repairing trenches. Farms occupied by H.Qrs + "B" Coy narrowly escaped destruction by "Jack Johnsons" which appeared to be searching for batteries close in rear. Weather fine. Some frost during night. No casualties.	

January. Page 7. Army Form C. 2118.

WAR DIARY
or
INTELLIGENCE SUMMARY.
(Erase heading not required.)

1st Battn The Gordon Highlanders.

Instructions regarding War Diaries and Intelligence Summaries are contained in F. S. Regs., Part II. and the Staff Manual respectively. Title pages will be prepared in manuscript.

1915.

Hour, Date, Place	Summary of Events and Information	Remarks and References to Appendices
January 20th in trenches near VIERSTRAAT.	Nothing of interest occurred. No casualties.	
January 21st in billets in LA CLYTTE.	Relieved in trenches by 2nd Suffolk Regt., and reached billets about 9.15 p.m. No casualties.	
January 22nd–24th do:	Nothing of note occurred except the arrival of six telephones ordered privately by the Commanding officer to replace the part. worn & unreliable instruments recently issued to the Battalion.	
January 25th in trenches near VIERSTRAAT	Left billets at 5 p.m. for the trenches where we took over the same line as usual from the 2nd Suffolk Regt. with the addition of 2 trenches on the right. No casualties.	

Instructions regarding War Diaries and Intelligence Summaries are contained in F. S. Regs., Part II. and the Staff Manual respectively. Title pages will be prepared in manuscript.

1915 -

WAR DIARY
or
INTELLIGENCE SUMMARY.
(Erase heading not required.)

January. Page 8 -

Army Form C. 2118.

1st Battn The Gordon Highlanders -

Hour, Date, Place	Summary of Events and Information	Remarks and References to Appendices
January 26th in trenches near VIERSTRAAT -	weather fine but cold - There was a light fall of snow in the evening - One man was killed & 5 men were wounded by snipers owing to the trenches newly taken over not being sufficiently traversed - This fault was remedied after dark & the men were employed as usual in improving & draining the trenches during the night.	
January 27th do:	hard frost. A few shells were fired at the house occupied by Battn Head Quarters but no damage done - no casualties. This day a draft of 166 men joined the Battn under the command of 2 Lieut C.S.J. Griffin. The bulk of the men, though of excellent physique, had had but a few months training. They were largely drawn from the miner class from Lanarkshire	

(9 29 6) W 2794 100,000 8/14 H W V Forms/C. 2118/11.

Army Form C. 2118.

WAR DIARY
or
INTELLIGENCE SUMMARY.
(*Erase heading not required.*)

January. Page 9.

1st Battn. The Gordon Highlanders.

1915.

Instructions regarding War Diaries and Intelligence Summaries are contained in F. S. Regs., Part II. and the Staff Manual respectively. Title pages will be prepared in manuscript.

Hour, Date, Place	Summary of Events and Information	Remarks and References to Appendices
January 27th (continued)	and that neighbourhood, but also included representatives from Canada, the United States, the Argentine & Shanghai.	
January 28th in trenches near VIERSTRAAT.	Hard frost. Battalion H.Q. was again shelled, one high-explosive shrapnel penetrating the part of the house occupied by ammunition carriers & orderlies, but no damage done beyond some greatcoats being torn to pieces & a bicycle smashed. Two men who were inside the room had a narrow escape. In one respect this was a remarkable day. A Staff Officer came round the trenches. This is the second occasion since November 1st 1914 on which a Staff Officer has visited the trenches occupied by the Battalion. Casualties - 1 man wounded.	

(9 29 6) W 2794 100,000 8/14 H W V Forms/C. 2118/11.

February. Page 1. Army Form C. 2118.

Instructions regarding War Diaries and Intelligence Summaries are contained in F. S. Regs., Part II. and the Staff Manual respectively. Title pages will be prepared in manuscript.

1915.

WAR DIARY or INTELLIGENCE SUMMARY.

(Erase heading not required.)

1st Battn The Gordon Highlanders.

Hour, Date, Place	Summary of Events and Information	Remarks and References to Appendices
February 1st In billets at LA CLYTTE.	This day the Battalion was issued with the blue "Balmoral" bonnet in place of the Glengarry - owing to the conspicuous nature of these new bonnets orders were issued that they were not to be worn in the trenches until khaki covers were received for them. Weather cold and wet.	
February 2nd In trenches near VIERSTRAAT.	The Battalion marched off at 5.15 p.m. for the trenches where we relieved the 2nd Suffolk Regt. fine day. no casualties.	
February 3rd Do:	Some Shelling. a few aeroplanes about. fine but windy. one man wounded by a stray bullet when working on the reserve line of trenches at night.	
February 4th Do:	a good deal of Shelling. Sky full of aeroplanes. 2 Lieut Erskine (4th A. & S. Highrs) (attached), saw with his glasses some Germans baling water out of their trenches. This was communicated to the artillery	

(9 29 6) W 2794 100,000 8/14 H W V Forms/C. 2118/11.

Instructions regarding War Diaries and Intelligence Summaries are contained in F. S. Regs., Part II. and the Staff Manual respectively. Title pages will be prepared in manuscript.

1915.

WAR DIARY
or
INTELLIGENCE SUMMARY.
(*Erase heading not required.*)

February. Page 2.

Army Form C. 2118.

1st Battn The Gordon Highlanders.

Hour, Date, Place	Summary of Events and Information	Remarks and References to Appendices
February 4th (contd) in trenches near VIERSTRAAT.	by telephone with the result that, after the usual ranging shots, a lyddite shell, followed in rapid succession by 3 others, was dropped into the middle of them. This incident proves the advantage to be gained by placing the officers in the front trenches in direct touch with the artillery. day fine. no casualties.	
February 5th do:	another fine day. usual shelling. 2 men wounded.	75
February 6th in billets in LA CLYTTE.	The 2nd Suffolk Regt relieved us in the trenches. The Battalion returned to billets where it arrived at 9.45 p.m. no casualties.	
February 7th - 9th do:	nothing of interest occurred. weather much improved.	
February 10th in trenches near VIERSTRAAT.	The Battalion left for the trenches at 6.15 p.m. where we relieved the 2nd Suffolk Regt as usual.	

Instructions regarding War Diaries and Intelligence Summaries are contained in F. S. Regs., Part II. and the Staff Manual respectively. Title pages will be prepared in manuscript.

1915.

WAR DIARY
or
INTELLIGENCE SUMMARY.
(Erase heading not required.)

February. Page 3. Army Form C. 2118.

1st Battn The Gordon Highlanders.

Hour, Date, Place	Summary of Events and Information	Remarks and References to Appendices
February 11th in trenches near VIERSTRAAT.	The Brigadier-General, General Staff, 2nd Army Corps, visited the trenches held by the Battalion, this being the 3rd visit since November 1st paid by any Staff officer to trenches held by the Battalion. (Apparently a tour of Inspection to the trenches is now technically described by the Staff as "Slumming".) fine day. no casualties.	
February 12th do:	a good deal of Shelling. very wet & misty. no casualties.	
February 13th do:	a certain amount of Shelling. a cold misty day. no casualties.	
February 14th in billets in LA CLYTTE.	A good deal of Shelling during the morning. At 4 p.m. our Batteries in rear opened a very heavy fire which was later ascertained to have been in support of the 28th Division who were 2 miles on our left. The Germans had attacked	75

(9 29 6) W 2794 100,000 8/14 H W V Forms/C. 2118/11.

February. Page 4.

Army Form C. 2118.

WAR DIARY
or
INTELLIGENCE SUMMARY. 1st Bn The Gordon Highlanders.
(*Erase heading not required.*)

Instructions regarding War Diaries and Intelligence Summaries are contained in F. S. Regs., Part II. and the Staff Manual respectively. Title pages will be prepared in manuscript.

1915.

Hour, Date, Place	Summary of Events and Information	Remarks and References to Appendices
February 14th (contd)	and taken one of their trenches but were later turned out by a counter-attack. In the evening the Battalion was relieved by the 2nd Suffolk Regt. A very cold wet day. No casualties. This was the 1st time the Battalion had done in the trenches without suffering any casualties, ~~this fact~~ being which was largely accounted for by the fact that the trenches had been put into a thoroughly defensible state by the 2nd Suffolks & ourselves. Nothing unusual occurred.	75
February 15th – 16th in billets in LA CLYTTE.		
February 17th in trenches near VIERSTRAAT.	The Battalion relieved the 2nd Suffolk Regt in the trenches in the evening. A draft of 16 men under the command of 2 Lieut H. Stuart-Menzies joined	

(9 29 6) W 2794 100,000 8/14 H W V Forms/C. 2118/11.

925.

Instructions regarding War Diaries and Intelligence Summaries are contained in F. S. Regs., Part II. and the Staff Manual respectively. Title pages will be prepared in manuscript.

WAR DIARY
or
INTELLIGENCE SUMMARY.
(*Erase heading not required.*)

1st Battn The Gordon Highlanders.

February - Page 5.

Army Form C. 2118.

Hour, Date, Place	Summary of Events and Information	Remarks and References to Appendices
February 17th (contd)	the Battalion. very wet. 2 men wounded.	
February 18th in trenches near VIERSTRAAT.	a quiet day. fine. 1 man killed by a sniper.	
February 19th do:	cold - some rain. In the evening the Battalion handed over part of the line of trenches it was holding to the 2nd Royal Scots, taking over in its place a trench known as K2 from the Honourable Artillery Company. This proved to be a very bad bargain as the trench taken over was found to be in a most deplorable condition. Such work as had been done on it appeared to have been largely devoted to the provision of shelters making the place somewhat resemble an Indian bazaar. These shelters were so placed as to reduce the fighting value	

Instructions regarding War Diaries and Intelligence Summaries are contained in F. S. Regs., Part II. and the Staff Manual respectively. Title pages will be prepared in manuscript.

WAR DIARY
or
INTELLIGENCE SUMMARY.
(*Erase heading not required.*)

February 1915. Page 7. 1st Bn Gordon Highlanders

Army Form C. 2118.

1915. Hour, Date, Place	Summary of Events and Information	Remarks and References to Appendices
February 22nd & 23rd In billets in LA CLYTTE.	Fine weather and frosty with mist in the morning usually up to 10.0 am. Nothing unusual occurred.	
February 24th in trenches near VIERSTRAAT.	The Battalion relieved 2nd Suffolk Regiment in Evening during a heavy fall of snow, relief complete by 10.30 pm. All night snow fell at intervals with intervals of bright moonlight which prevented much movement in the trenches. A quiet night and no casualties.	
Feby 25th in trenches near VIERSTRAAT.	Fine day, K.2 + L.1 trenches were shelled at intervals during day, two shells landing in the former but no damage was done. At night one Corporal was killed and 3 Ptes wounded by snipers. Bright moonlight and a mist allowed considerable works to be done during the night.	
Feby 26th in trenches near VIERSTRAAT.	Heavy mist in morning which cleared about mid day. Hostile artillery again shelled K.2 but did no material damage. One Sergeant + one Pte killed by rifle fire. Inter company reliefs took place this night without casualty.	

(9 29 6) W 2794 100,000 8/14 H W V Forms/C. 2118/11.

Instructions regarding War Diaries and Intelligence Summaries are contained in F. S. Regs., Part II. and the Staff Manual respectively. Title pages will be prepared in manuscript.

or

~~INTELLIGENCE SUMMARY.~~ 1st Bn: The Gordon Highlanders.

(Erase heading not required.)

Hour, Date, Place	Summary of Events and Information	Remarks and References to Appendices
1st to 4th March 1915. LA CLYTTE.	In rest billets. [dull and rainy weather.] On evening of 4th March relieved 2nd Suffolks in trenches (Section K2 & L) near VIERSTRAAT. Relief complete by 9.0 pm without casualty. O.C. 4th Gordon Hrs. accompanied Bn HQ and "B" Coy 4th Gordon Highrs was attached for instruction in trench duties, one platoon going to each Company. Quiet night.	
5th March 1915 trenches near VIERSTRAAT. (Section K2 & L)	[Dull day with some rain. Owing to Farm occupied by Bn HQ having been shelled during previous 4 days another Farm 400 yds. further South was selected as Bn. HQ by day.] K2 trench received some shelling but damage immaterial. 4th Gordon Highrs maxim gun was brought up in reserve. 3 men killed during night	
6th March 1915 trenches near VIERSTRAAT	Dull and rainy. Quiet day and night. Inter Company reliefs were carried out. 2 Casualties. Quiet night.	
7th March 1915	Dull. L.6 trench rather heavily shelled, the parapet	

(9 29 6) W 2794 100,000 8/14 H W V Forms/C. 2118/11.

Instructions regarding War Diaries and Intelligence Summaries are contained in F. S. Regs., Part II. and the Staff Manual respectively. Title pages will be prepared in manuscript.

~~INTELLIGENCE~~ SUMMARY. 1st Bn. The Gordon Highlanders.

(*Erase heading not required.*)

Hour, Date, Place	Summary of Events and Information	Remarks and References to Appendices
7th March. 1915 (contd) trenches near VIERSTRAAT	being knocked down in 2 places, one shell landed in L.1. wounding two men. Quiet afternoon and night.	
8th March 1915 trenches near VIERSTRAAT	Very cold with strong N. wind and snow at intervals. In the morning some shelling by our own guns but enemy quiet. About 4 pm German shrapnel burst in front of Reserve farm killing 2 and wounding 7 men. Relieved by 2nd Suffolk Regt; relief complete 9.30 pm.	75
9th to 11th March 1915. in billets at LA CLYTTE.	Fine weather but cold - nothing noteworthy occurred. At 9.0 pm on 11th inst. orders received that Battalion is Divisional Reserve & to be ready to turn out at 1 hour's notice. Quiet night.	
12th March 1915 in billets at LA CLYTTE.	Fine weather, quiet day. Relieved 2nd Suffolk Regt. relief complete 9.45 pm. 1 Coy 4th Bn Gordon Hrs attached, one platoon going to each Company for instruction. Quiet night. 5 men wounded.	

Instructions regarding War Diaries and Intelligence Summaries are contained in F. S. Regs., Part II. and the Staff Manual respectively. Title pages will be prepared in manuscript.

Army Form C. 2118.

WAR DIARY
or
~~INTELLIGENCE SUMMARY.~~ 1st Bn. The Gordon Highlanders.
(Erase heading not required.)

Hour, Date, Place	Summary of Events and Information	Remarks and references to Appendices
1st April. 1915. In trenches (N) North of VIERSTRAAT	Warm and sunny day. Exceptionally quiet (Bismarck's birthday). Orders received that we are to move again. This time to "K" Sector. ~~Quiet night one man wounded.~~	
2nd April 1915. In trenches (N) North of VIERSTRAAT	Warm with some rain. at night inter Company reliefs took place without casualty. [WORCESTERSHIRE Regiment officers reconnoitred trenches in Evening. Quiet night no casualties.	
3rd April 1915. In trenches (N) North of VIERSTRAAT.	Some rain. Quiet day and night.	
4th April. 1915.	Rain. Relieved in Evening by WORCESTERSHIRE Regiment. relief complete 10 am no casualties. Right half Bn. took over part of "K" and "J" Sectors (K1. - K1A. 5.6 & J.11) their relief complete 11.45 pm	
5th April 1915.	Left half Bn. in billets at LA CLYTTE. Quiet day and night in the trenches.	
6th April 1915.	Captains G.I.R. Hume Gore and D.P. Turnbull DSO and 110 rank & file arrived as re-inforcement. All quiet in the trenches.	
7th April. 1915.	Rainy day. all quiet.	
8th April 1915.	Major P.W. Brown. arrived and took over Command from Major A.W.F Baird CMG. DSO. All quiet.	

Army Form C. 2118.

Instructions regarding War Diaries and Intelligence Summaries are contained in F. S. Regs., Part II. and the Staff Manual respectively. Title pages will be prepared in manuscript.

WAR DIARY
or
~~INTELLIGENCE SUMMARY.~~ 1st Bn. The Gordon Highlanders.

(Erase heading not required.)

Hour, Date, Place	Summary of Events and Information	Remarks and references to Appendices
16th April 1915.	Fine day. K1. again shelled in afternoon but no damage. Two men wounded during the day. Right Half Bn. relieved Left Half in evening without casualty. Relief complete 10.30pm. Quiet night.	
17th April 1915.	Left Half Bn. in Billets at LA CLYTTE. Mine under Hill 60. exploded at 7.0 pm. Quiet day and night.	
18th April 1915.	Quiet day in trenches. Lieuts C. Cochrane and J. Mackay and 102 men arrived as reinforcement. Quiet night	
19th April 1915.	Quiet day + night in trenches and billets.	
20th April 1915	" " " " " " "	
21st April 1915	" " " " " " "	
22nd April 1915	Left half Bn. relieved Right half in trenches. Relief complete without casualty by 9.40pm. Germans on our immediate right, reported to be using asphyxiating gas. Some men of right Half Bn complained of sore eyes by day probably due to this gas. Pieces of cloth and tins for water were sent to trenches as remedy was reported to be a wet cloth held over face. (1 man killed. Quiet night.	

(9 29 6) W4141—463 100,000 9/14 H W V Forms/C. 2118/10

Page 4.

Army Form C. 2118.

Instructions regarding War Diaries and Intelligence Summaries are contained in F. S. Regs., Part II. and the Staff Manual respectively. Title pages will be prepared in manuscript.

WAR DIARY
or
~~INTELLIGENCE SUMMARY.~~ 1st Bn. The Gordon Highlanders –

(*Erase heading not required.*)

Hour, Date, Place	Summary of Events and Information	Remarks and references to Appendices
23rd April 1915.	Right Half Bn. in Billets at LA CLYTTE – Quiet day on our front but heavy firing from direction of YPRES where French were reported to have given way. Orders received at noon for Major P.W. Brown to take over command of 6th Territorial Battalion Gordon Highlanders and to leave for that duty at once – Major A.W.F. Baird CMG. DSO. accordingly re-assumed command – Cold N. wind – Quiet night – no casualties –	
24th April 1915.	Cold N.E. wind – Message from Artillery received in Evening that German artillery had been registering on all trenches "H" to "L". Accordingly, as attack seemed probable, the Right Half Bn. from LA CLYTTE was ordered up and the trenches reinforced by 64 men. Quiet night – no casualties –	
25th April 1915.	Heavy bombarding continues N. of YPRES but quiet on our front – Right Half Bn. withdrawn to LA CLYTTE but extra garrison of 44 men kept in trenches – 2nd Lieut. O. Horsley and 106 men arrived in afternoon as reinforcement. Quiet day and night – no casualties –	

(9 29 6) W4141—463 100,000 9/14 H W V Forms/C. 2118/10

Army Form C. 2118.

Instructions regarding War Diaries and Intelligence Summaries are contained in F. S. Regs., Part II. and the Staff Manual respectively. Title pages will be prepared in manuscript.

WAR DIARY
or
~~INTELLIGENCE~~ ~~SUMMARY.~~
(*Erase heading not required.*)

1st Bn. The Gordon Highlanders.

Hour, Date, Place	Summary of Events and Information	Remarks and references to Appendices
26th April 1915.	Heavy cannonading continues northwards, otherwise quiet day and night. No casualties.	
27th April 1915.	Cold and Cloudy. Quiet day and night. 2 men wounded.	
28th April 1915.	Fine and warm. 1 man wounded during day. Right half Bn. relieved Left Half Bn., relief complete without casualty by 9.45 pm. J11 trench was handed over to ROYAL SCOTS and K.1.B trench taken over from 4th Bn. Gordon Highrs (T.F). Quiet night.	
29th April 1915.	Left Half Bn. in Billets at LA CLYTTE. Quiet day. Captain R.O. Blair Cunynghame was wounded in head about 10 pm by German Bullet. By night Germans were somewhat active with rifle grenades, one of which killed one man and wounded five. During the day in LA CLYTTE 2nd Lieut J.H. Plummer was wounded in practicing with hand grenade	
30th April 1915.	Quiet day and night in trenches. One man wounded.	Casualties – month K 3 W. 2 + 10

1 Gordons.
April 1915
Brasserie

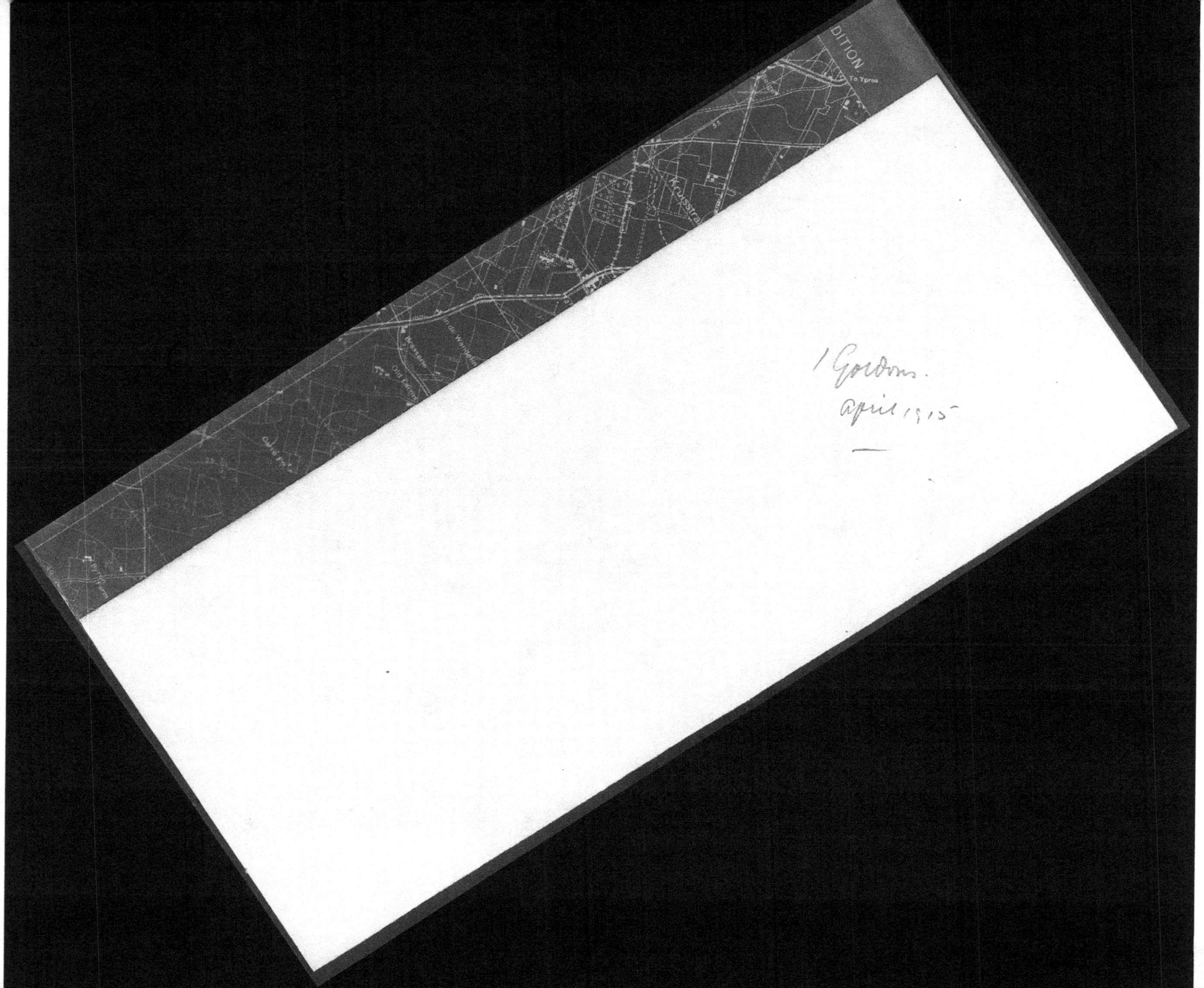

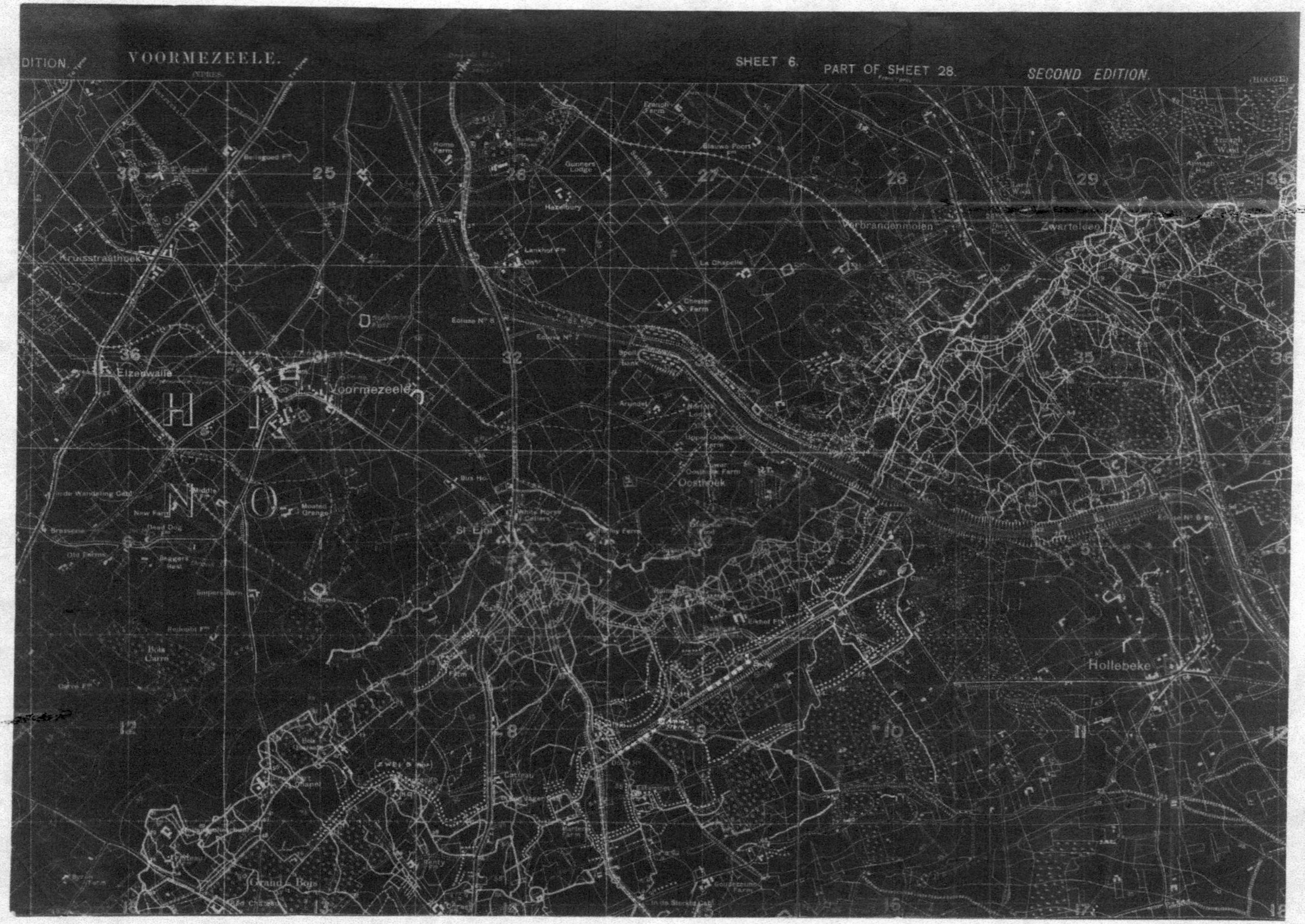
DITION.
VOORMEZEELE.
SHEET 6.
PART OF SHEET 28.
SECOND EDITION.
Kruisstraathoek
Elzenwalle
Voormezeele
Verbrandenmolen
Zwarteleen
Oosthoek
St Eloi
Hollebeke
Grand Bois
La Chapelle
Hazebury
H
I
N
O

/ Gordon.
April 1915

Instructions regarding War Diaries and Intelligence Summaries are contained in F. S. Regs., Part II. and the Staff Manual respectively. Title pages will be prepared in manuscript.

WAR DIARY
or
INTELLIGENCE ~~SUMMARY~~. 1st Bn. The Gordon Highlanders

(Erase heading not required.)

Hour, Date, Place	Summary of Events and Information	Remarks and references to Appendices
28th May 1915. HOOGE.	Some shelling of our trenches in the morning, but no damage done. Posts were established by night along the main road as far as HOOGE to join up with cavalry. Quiet night.	
29th May 1915. HOOGE.	Some more shelling in the morning, otherwise quiet. By night a new trench was dug N. of YPRES-MENIN road and occupied by 1 platoon. Quiet night.	
30th May 1915. HOOGE.	Quiet day and night. Inter Company Reliefs.	
31st May 1915 HOOGE	Quiet day and night beyond the usual shelling of the cross roads and main tracks.	Cas 1 month 1 K. 5 W. 26.

Instructions regarding War Diaries and Intelligence Summaries are contained in F. S. Regs., Part II. and the Staff Manual respectively. Title pages will be prepared in manuscript.

Page 1. Army Form C. 2118.

WAR DIARY
or
~~INTELLIGENCE SUMMARY.~~ 1st Bn. The Gordon Highlanders –

(Erase heading not required.)

Hour, Date, Place	Summary of Events and Information	Remarks and references to Appendices
1st June. 1915. HOOGE	Some shelling in the morning, otherwise a quiet day and night –	
2nd June. 1915. HOOGE.	Very heavy shelling commenced at 6.30 am and with the exception of a short break of 3/4 of an hour about midday, the bombardment continued all day, HOOGE Village itself coming in for the largest share (contd on Page 2)	

(9 29 6) W 4141—463 100,000 9/14 H W V Forms/C. 2118/10

Army Form C. 2118.

Instructions regarding War Diaries and Intelligence Summaries are contained in F. S. Regs., Part II. and the Staff Manual respectively. Title pages will be prepared in manuscript.

WAR DIARY
or
~~INTELLIGENCE~~ SUMMARY. 1st Bn. The Gordon Highlanders.
(Erase heading not required.)

Hour, Date, Place	Summary of Events and Information	Remarks and references to Appendices
2nd June 1915 (Contd) HOOGE.	Small reply was made by our artillery to the enemy's fire. 22 men were killed and 46 wounded and 2/Lieut Bothwell slightly wounded by Shrapnel. Companies were relieved by Companies in Support. Quiet night but much work was required to repair the damage caused by the German high explosive shells.	
3rd June 1915. HOOGE.	Quiet morning. Some shelling of our line in the afternoon but no damage done. Quiet night.	
4th June 1915. HOOGE.	Quiet day but rifle fire by night was heavier than usual probably due to enemy trying to interrupt our working parties N. of YPRES-MENIN road where a further new trench was built.	
5th June 1915.	Quiet day but rifle fire still heavier than usual by night.	
6th June 1915.	Quiet day. By night German trench mortars were very busy round HOOGE. By day they had been silenced by our artillery.	

Instructions regarding War Diaries and Intelligence Summaries are contained in F. S. Regs., Part II. and the Staff Manual respectively. Title pages will be prepared in manuscript.

Page. 3.

Army Form C. 2118.

WAR DIARY
or
~~INTELLIGENCE~~ SUMMARY. 1st Gordon Highlanders

(Erase heading not required.)

Hour, Date, Place	Summary of Events and Information	Remarks and references to Appendices
7th June 1915. HOOGE.	Quiet day. Orders received that Bn. will be relieved by 2nd Suffolk Regt. on night of 8/9 June 1915. Suffolk officers came up by night to reconnoitre trenches. Quiet night.	
8th June 1915. HOOGE.	Quiet day with some shelling round Bn. HQ. during the afternoon. Relieved by Suffolk Regt. in evening, relief complete 12.10 am. and Bn. marched back to bivouac between POPERINGHE and VLAMERTINGHE.	
9th June 1915. in Bivouac.	Quiet day. One Officer and a selected private ~~were~~ sent from each Coy. to attend a "gass" class and they afterwards went through the process of being gassed. The smoke helmets combined with the respirators were found to form an efficient antidote.	

(9 29 6) W4141—463 100,000 9/14 H W V Forms/C. 2118/10

Army Form C. 2118.

Instructions regarding War Diaries and Intelligence Summaries are contained in F. S. Regs., Part II. and the Staff Manual respectively. Title pages will be prepared in manuscript.

WAR DIARY
or
~~INTELLIGENCE~~ SUMMARY. 1st Battn The Gordon Highlanders

(*Erase heading not required.*)

Hour, Date, Place	Summary of Events and Information	Remarks and references to Appendices
10th June 1915 in Bivouac at Brandhoek	Quiet day – The whole day was given to completing the men in equipment etc. The Commanding Officer announced that "Distinguished Conduct Medals" had been awarded to two men of the Battalion. (No 5871 / 2506 Heavy rain fell during the night	R. Q.M. Sgt G. Farrant / Lance Corporal D. Hart.)
11th June 1915 in Bivouac at Brandhoek	The Commanding Officer inspected the Coys: and the Battn had a route march in the afternoon.	
12th June 1915 in Bivouac at Brandhoek	Church parade in the morning. Quiet day.	
13th June 1915	Printed copies of instructions were issued to each man. The Battn moved up to the town of YPRES and billeted there. All quiet.	

(9 29 6) W4141—463 100,000 9/14 H W V Forms/C. 2118/10

Instructions regarding War Diaries and Intelligence Summaries are contained in F. S. Regs., Part II. and the Staff Manual respectively. Title pages will be prepared in manuscript.

WAR DIARY

~~or~~

~~INTELLIGENCE SUMMARY~~

(Erase heading not required.)

Army Form C. 2118.

Hour, Date, Place	Summary of Events and Information	Remarks and references to Appendices
YPRES. 15th June (cont)	respirators were used, which proved effective and although some men were rather bad, no one was so overcome that they could not keep on. Trenches were occupied at about 1am 16th June.	
16th June.	Many wounded of other units were found in trenches but all were sent back or brought under cover. LT ERSKINE (4th Argyll & Sutherland Highlanders) (attached) discovered that trenches 250 yards to our front were unoccupied. It was decided to occupy them at dusk, and this was done without any opposition.	
17th June.	Bn Head Quarters and 2 reserve companies (C and D) were heavily shelled all day and had about 80 casualties. Heard that we should be relieved by 9th KRR (New Army). Trenches much improved during night and approaches blocked by LTs ERSKINE and HORSLEY with bomb throwers. Several gas shells used by enemy.	
18th June	Fairly quiet day were relieved about 10 pm and returned to bivouack in BRANDHOEK arriving there about 3am	

Instructions regarding War Diaries and Intelligence Summaries are contained in F. S. Regs., Part II. and the Staff Manual respectively. Title pages will be prepared in manuscript.

WAR DIARY
~~or~~
~~INTELLIGENCE SUMMARY~~
(Erase heading not required.)

Army Form C. 2118.

Hour, Date, Place	Summary of Events and Information	Remarks and references to Appendices
BRANDHOEK.		
23rd June (continued)	Wrestling on Horseback 1st	
	Bomb throwing (Team competition) 1st	
	Mounted Tug of War 2nd	
	Throwing the hammer 2nd & 3rd.	
	Bomb throwing (individual) 2nd	
	Putting the shot. 2nd	
	Pillow fighting 3rd	
24th June	General Haldane presented DCM to QMS FARRANT.	
	Quiet day. Route march by companies in morning, and lecture by C.O. to Officers & NCOs	
	Captain Bartholomew re-joined from sick leave.	
25th June.	Quiet Day. Capt H P T Burn. Capt L Gordon and Capt C Ogston awarded Distinguished Service Order. Capt J Bartholomew and Lt J L Cruickshank awarded Military Cross (Royal Flying Corps)	
26th June.	~~Church~~ Draft of 93 NCOs and men arrived including 6 machine gunners and 11 signallers – Concert in evening.	
27th June	Church Parade at 10.15 am – quiet day.	

1247 W 3299 200,000 (E) 8/14 J.B.C. & A. Forms/C. 2118/11.

Instructions regarding War Diaries and Intelligence Summaries are contained in F. S. Regs., Part II. and the Staff Manual respectively. Title pages will be prepared in manuscript.

WAR DIARY or INTELLIGENCE SUMMARY.

(Erase heading not required.)

Army Form C. 2118.

1st Bn Gordon Highlanders

Hour, Date, Place	Summary of Events and Information	Remarks and references to Appendices
1st July 1915 BRANDHOEK.	Two hand carts were received from Bde, for carrying rations etc to the trenches. They should be the means of saving many casualties in ration parties in future. Fine day.	
2nd July 1915 BRANDHOEK.	Companies route marched in morning - very hot day.	
3rd July 1915 BRANDHOEK	Major A W F Baird CMG. DSO. was appointed liaison officer GHQ.	
	quiet day very hot	
4th July 1915 BRANDHOEK	Church parade in morning Lt A L Davidson 2/Lt D MacNaughton and J MacKay proceeded on leave of absence for four days	
5th July 1915 BRANDHOEK	Quiet day ~~five~~ seven NCOs and men went on leave	

(9 29 6) W4141—463 100,000 9/14 H W V Forms/C. 2118/10

Army Form C. 2118.

Instructions regarding War Diaries and Intelligence Summaries are contained in F. S. Regs., Part II. and the Staff Manual respectively. Title pages will be prepared in manuscript.

WAR DIARY
or
INTELLIGENCE SUMMARY.
(Erase heading not required.)

Hour, Date, Place	Summary of Events and Information	Remarks and references to Appendices
BRANDHOEK.		
6th July 1915.	Companies (A+B) practised assault. C+D route march very hot day	
7th July	The following officers arrived 2nd Lts. R K GORDON. J A H. BROWN. V A BERRY. Quiet day	
8th July	Three NCO's granted leave of absence. Arm drill and musketry parades	
9th July.	Battalion Route march (10 miles) Cookers were taken and dinners issued on the way..	
10th July.	CO and Company Commanders inspected trenches which the battalion was taking over on night 11th.	

(9 29 6) W 4141—463 100,000 9/14 H W V Forms/C. 2118/10

Instructions regarding War Diaries and Intelligence Summaries are contained in F. S. Regs., Part II. and the Staff Manual respectively. Title pages will be prepared in manuscript.

Army Form C. 2118.

WAR DIARY
or
INTELLIGENCE SUMMARY.
(Erase heading not required.)

Hour, Date, Place	Summary of Events and Information	Remarks and references to Appendices
BRANDHOEK.		
11th July 1915.	Church parade in morning.	
	Lieut. T.B. Erskine received the Military Cross. Quiet day.	
12th July	Lieut Colonel P.W. Brown arrived and took over command from Capt H.P. Burn DSO.	
6.0 pm	Battalion left for the trenches and relieved the 1st Royal Irish Rifles 7th Infantry Brigade	
	Relief completed at 1.45am without any Casualties	
	Trenches were situated in HOOGE and to the West and South of it. This being the most Easterly point of the YPRES Salient. Quiet night.	
13th.	Uneventful day. Enemy fired a few trench mortars without doing any serious damage	
	Casualties 1 Killed 5 wounded (1 officer)	
14th.	Fine in the morning. trenches had been considerably improved during the night, and made in a better sanitary condition. Brigadier and Divisional Commander visited Battalion H.Q. The former went around the trenches.	
	Wet night	
15th.	Several more Snipers posts were established with good results. 450 Express Rifle did good work on enemy's loopholes. "D" Company's dug-outs were shelled in afternoon	
	No Casualties	
16th.	Very Quiet day – enemy's Snipers practically silenced. our Snipers think they have accounted for about 10 Germans.	
17th.	Showery all day with strong S.W. wind towards evening. Enemy still very quiet on our front, but working hard at night. Several of their parties were fired into during the night. Casualties 3 wounded	

Army Form C. 2118.

WAR DIARY
or
INTELLIGENCE SUMMARY.
(Erase heading not required.)

Instructions regarding War Diaries and Intelligence Summaries are contained in F. S. Regs., Part II. and the Staff Manual respectively. Title pages will be prepared in manuscript.

Hour, Date, Place	Summary of Events and Information	Remarks and References to Appendices
19th July (continued)	and machine gunners, amounted to killed 9 wounded 34 and included Lieut T B ERSKINE 4th Argyl and Sutherland Highlanders who was killed: this officer was transferred to the Gordon Highlanders in a Gazette a few days later - his loss was mourned deeply by the battalion, with all ranks of which he was a favourite. 2/Lt Horsley who was in charge of the snipers was also wounded.	
20th July - HOOGE trenches.	Orders were received for the battalion to return to the HOOGE trenches in relief of the Middlesex Regt which had lost about 100 casualties. A company proceeded by daylight to the trenches, and took over the crater and captured GERMAN trench, the other companies arriving about 10 pm. The trenches were very heavily shelled during the afternoon, evening and early part of the night, and were considerably knocked about - at one time it appeared as though an attempt by	

(9 29 6) W 2794 100,000 8/14 H W V Forms/C. 2118/11.

Instructions regarding War Diaries and Intelligence Summaries are contained in F. S. Regs., Part II. and the Staff Manual respectively. Title pages will be prepared in manuscript.

Army Form C. 2118.

WAR DIARY
or
INTELLIGENCE SUMMARY.
(Erase heading not required.)

Hour, Date, Place	Summary of Events and Information	Remarks and references to Appendices
HOOGE trenches 20th July (continued)	the Germans to recapture their lost trenches was imminent, but beyond heavy shelling the attack did not materialize. About 1am the shelling practically ceased and the remainder of the night was spent in repairing the damage done. Lieut G. McCallum and 2nd Lt A. R. Davidson were wounded, other casualties were killed 12 wounded 32	
21st July HOOGE (trenches)	Much quieter but a certain amount of shelling all day, especially from the enemy's trench mortars. Position much strengthened during the night. Casualties 3 killed 16 wounded.	
22nd July HOOGE (trenches)	Quieter day than yesterday - very wet. German trench mortars still fairly active. Relieved in evening by 7th Rifle Brigade. Owing to wet weather relief was not completed until 3.20 am.	See 8th Bde O.O. No 3 d/22.7.15

(9 29 6) W 4141—463 100,000 9/14 H W V Forms/C. 2118/10

Army Form C. 2118.

Instructions regarding War Diaries and Intelligence Summaries are contained in F. S. Regs., Part II. and the Staff Manual respectively. Title pages will be prepared in manuscript.

WAR DIARY
or
INTELLIGENCE SUMMARY.
(Erase heading not required.)

Hour, Date, Place	Summary of Events and Information	Remarks and references to Appendices
23rd July BRANDHOEK - bivouac.	Quiet day which was spent in cleaning up.	
24th July BRANDHOEK.	Left for new trenches at 6.40pm and relieved the Manchester Regiment in trenches I 34 C. Relief completed without casualties at 12.25am 25 inst. Trenches fair, and dug outs in reserve very comfortable	See 8th Bde O.O. No 5 d/24.7.15
25th July. trenches near VERBRANDENMOLEN.	Owing to wet weather trenches were flooded in parts but were drained with success. An excellent view of the surrounding country and enemy's trenches can be obtained from the Bluff, a portion of rising ground which we hold.	

(9 29 6) W4141—463 100,000 9/14 H W V Forms/C. 2118/10.

Instructions regarding War Diaries and Intelligence Summaries are contained in F. S. Regs., Part II. and the Staff Manual respectively. Title pages will be prepared in manuscript.

Army Form C. 2118.

WAR DIARY
or
INTELLIGENCE SUMMARY.
(Erase heading not required.)

Hour, Date, Place	Summary of Events and Information	Remarks and references to Appendices
VERBRANDEN HOLEN. 26 July 1915 – trenches	Divisional and Brigade commanders visited the trenches which had dried up considerably since the rain. In the evening at about 7pm the enemy exploded a mine in T sector about a mile to our ~~left~~ right, without doing any damage.	
27th July – trenches	Quiet day, new portion of trench was taken over S of canal by A company who had some good opportunities for sniping. 2nd Lieut F.G. Stronach shot through the head and died at 11.15pm.	
28th July – trenches	Quiet day, strong westerly wind which helped to dry the ground after the recent showers. 2nd Lieut Stronach was buried at Chester Farm at 7.30pm. A mine exploded on our right at about 8pm presumably German, but nothing came of it.	

(9 29 6) W4141—463 100,000 9/14 H W V Forms/C. 2118/10

Army Form C. 2118.

Instructions regarding War Diaries and Intelligence Summaries are contained in F. S. Regs., Part II. and the Staff Manual respectively. Title pages will be prepared in manuscript.

WAR DIARY
or
INTELLIGENCE SUMMARY.
(Erase heading not required.)

Hour, Date, Place	Summary of Events and Information	Remarks and references to Appendices
VERBRANDENMOLEN. 29th July. - trenches	Fine day - enemy shelled the Bluff, but were silenced by the Belgian Artillery who were supporting us.	
30th July - trenches	At 2.30 am a very heavy bombardment on our left in the direction of HOOGE; everything quiet to our front - later news arrived that 9th Rifle Brigade had been driven from trenches on either side of the crater in HOOGE, the exact position we had been holding before we came to our present trenches. A counter attack was being organised. A good deal of artillery fire during the day, all in the same direction, but no losses.	

(9 29 6) W4141—463 100,000 9/14 H W V Forms/C. 2118/10

Instructions regarding War Diaries and Intelligence Summaries are contained in F. S. Regs., Part II. and the Staff Manual respectively. Title pages will be prepared in manuscript.

Army Form C. 2118.

WAR DIARY
or
INTELLIGENCE SUMMARY.
(Erase heading not required.)

Hour, Date, Place	Summary of Events and Information	Remarks and references to Appendices
31st July HERBRANDENHOEK Trenches	Report arrived that enemy had gained a footing in ZOUAVE WOOD but had been driven out and that we were holding the northern edge; everything quiet in our own district. Heavy bombardment at intervals during the day, but no result was reported.	

[illegible]
Lt Col
Cmdg 1st Gordon Highlanders.

(9 29 6) W 4141—463 100,000 9/14 H W V Forms/C. 2118/10

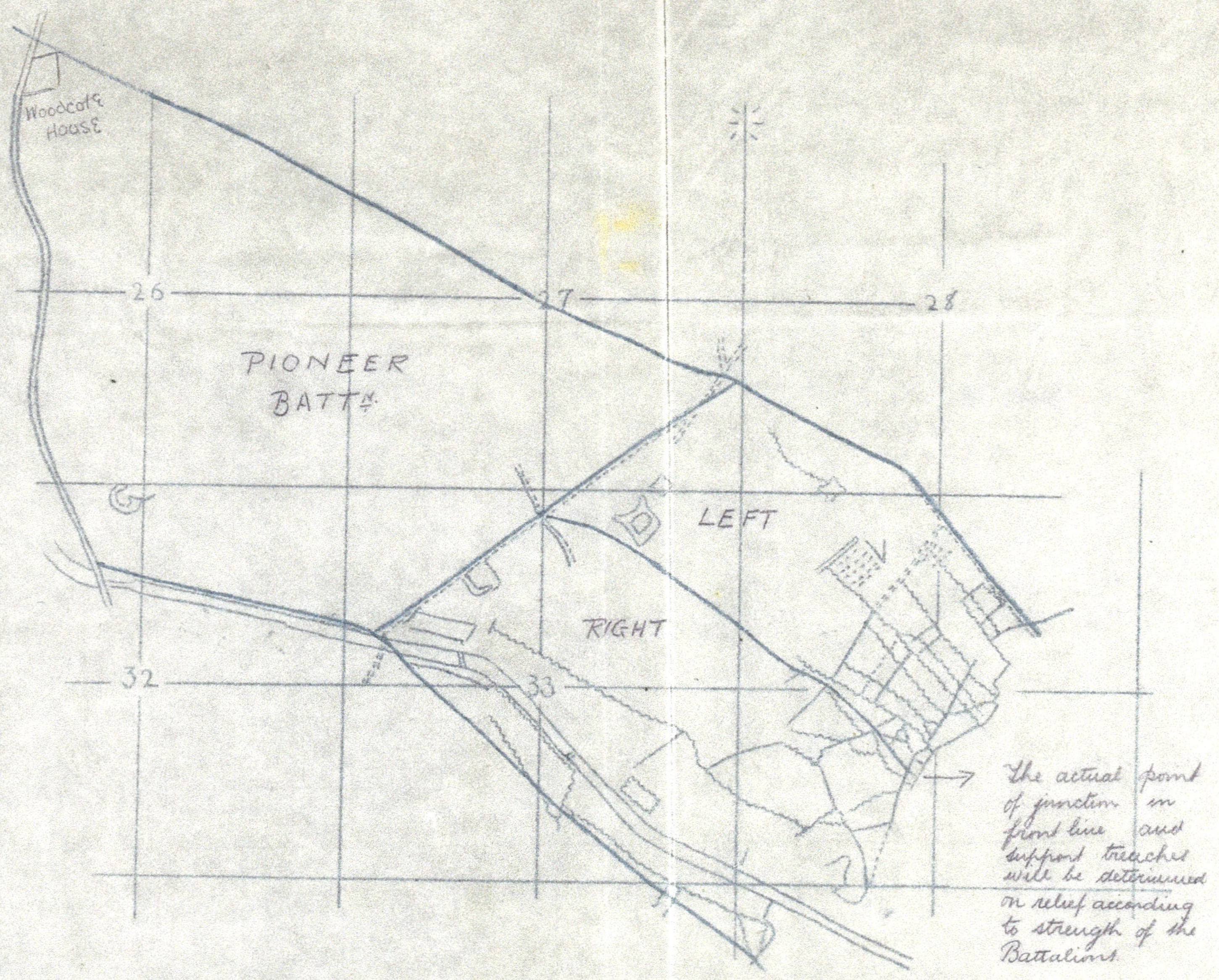
Woodcote House
26
27
28
PIONEER BATTn.
LEFT
RIGHT
32
33
The actual point of junction in front line and support trenches will be determined on relief according to strength of the Battalions

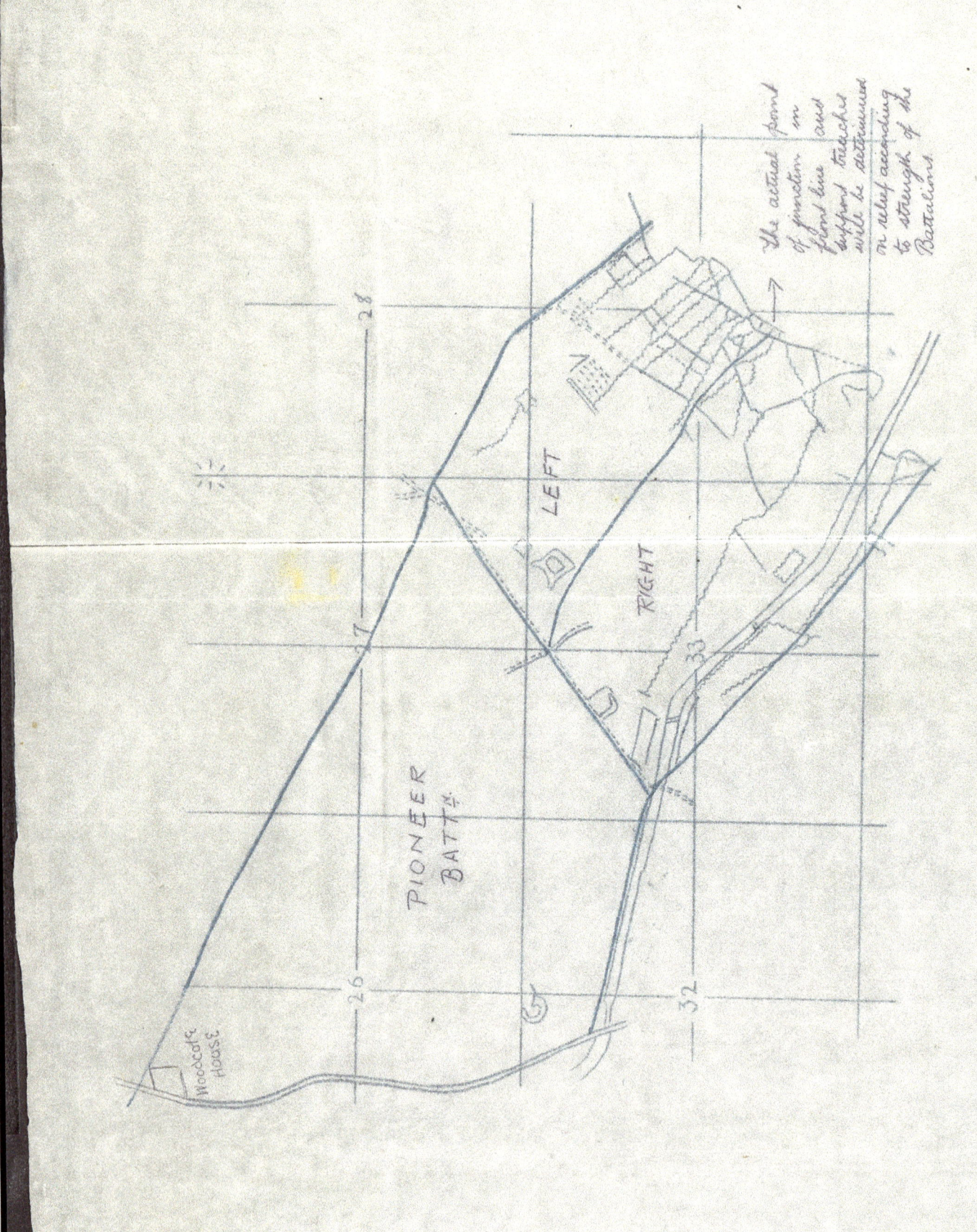

1st Gordon Highlanders. 2. August 1915.

Army Form C. 2118.

WAR DIARY
or
INTELLIGENCE SUMMARY.
(Erase heading not required.)

Instructions regarding War Diaries and Intelligence Summaries are contained in F. S. Regs., Part II. and the Staff Manual respectively. Title pages will be prepared in manuscript.

Hour, Date, Place	Summary of Events and Information	Remarks and references to Appendices
4th August (continued)	"Colonel Ross, Officers, noncommissioned officers & men it gives me great pleasure to see such a fine battalion on parade today – You only came out of the trenches last night and the smart & soldierlike manner in which you have turned out reflects the greatest credit on you all – Your commanding officer informs me that you have not had such a strenuous time in these last trenches as you had at HOOGE: there you had a very hard time of it and I want to thank you for the very fine work you did – The attack by the grenadiers of the battalion on 19th July was splendidly carried out – Again you have shown yourselves worthy representatives of that famous regiment, the Gordon Highlanders."	
5th August. Same bivouac.	Inspection of companies by C.O. in morning – Drums (4 side + 1 big) which had just been issued were played with the pipes in the evening to everyone's enjoyment –	

1st Gordon Highlanders. 5. August 1915. Army Form C. 2118.

WAR DIARY
or
INTELLIGENCE SUMMARY.
(Erase heading not required.)

Instructions regarding War Diaries and Intelligence Summaries are contained in F. S. Regs., Part II. and the Staff Manual respectively. Title pages will be prepared in manuscript.

Hour, Date, Place	Summary of Events and Information	Remarks and references to Appendices
20th to 22nd August. (Continued)	retaliation by the enemy: we were very lucky however & had few casualties – one of our machine guns was damaged by a shell on 22nd.	
23rd August. Same trenches.	Quiet day – battalion was relieved in evening, relief being completed by 11.10 pm. 5th Bn Sherwood Foresters took over Battalion H.Q. and reserve dug outs. 6th Bn Sherwood Foresters took over trenches 28 & 29 and the 7th Bn Sherwood Foresters trench 30. Casualties during the fortnight's stay in the trenches were 2 officers wounded, 8 other ranks killed & 26 wounded.	8th Bde Operation Order No 6. 1st Gordon Highrs O. O. No 1.
24th to 27th August. Bivouac near OUDERDOM.	Days devoted to cleaning up, baths, inspections and parades – 3rd Divisional band played on 2 occasions near the bivouac –	
28th August. Same bivouac.	Brigade Sports were held, the battalion being successful in the following events – Horsejump – 1st; Mounted wrestling 1st; Tug of war 2nd; Mile 2nd –	

(9 29 6) W4141—463 100,000 9/14 H W V Forms/C. 2118/10

1st Bn Gordon Highlanders. **WAR DIARY** *or* **INTELLIGENCE SUMMARY** *(Erase heading not required.)* September 1915. Army Form C. 2118

Instructions regarding War Diaries and Intelligence Summaries are contained in F. S. Regs., Part II. and the Staff Manual respectively. Title Pages will be prepared in manuscript.

Place	Date	Hour	Summary of Events and Information	Remarks and references to Appendices
Bivouac at Farm H19C.0.3	1st Sept.		Battalion was inspected by General Sir Herbert Plumer, Comdg. 2nd Army, who expressed his great pleasure in seeing such a fine body of men on parade. He remarked on the steadiness in the ranks and clean and smart appearance of all. Captain G.M. Monteith rejoined and took over command of C company. The battalion was equipped with the new khaki Balmoral bonnet, to which was added a rosette of Gordon tartan and the regimental cap badge.	
Bivouac at Farm H13.D.5.5.	2nd Sept.		Moved bivouac about 500 yards to another farm near VLAMERTINGHE on account of 3rd Division billeting area being once more changed. Very heavy rain all afternoon and night which was most unfortunate when move was taking place.	
D°	3rd Sept.		Another day of heavy rain and, as there was no shelter beyond bivouacs of waterproof sheets and canvas, a most unpleasant day was spent. No one has yet been able to explain why, after holding the YPRES salient for over a year, no accomodation has yet been provided for troops who are supposed to be resting.	

1st Bn Gordon Highlanders. 3 **WAR DIARY** or **INTELLIGENCE SUMMARY** September 1915. Army Form C. 2118

(Erase heading not required.)

Instructions regarding War Diaries and Intelligence Summaries are contained in F. S. Regs., Part II. and the Staff Manual respectively. Title Pages will be prepared in manuscript.

Place	Date	Hour	Summary of Events and Information	Remarks and references to Appendices
Same bivouac.	6th to 11th Sept.		Ordinary training, route marches, musketry and bathing parades at DICKEBUSCH. Weather much warmer. Sports were concluded on 6th: On 8th Maj. General A. Haldane, CB, DSO, Comdg 3rd Division, presented the ribbon of the D.C.M. to No 7765, L/Sgt. W. Smith. – Same working parties on 8th as on 4th. On 11th Grenade and Machine Gun sections went up to trench line on hill of HOOGE to take over posts during daylight of 12th.	
HOOGE trenches I.18.B.	12th Sept.		Relieved 3rd Bn Worcester Regiment in HOOGE trenches – dispositions were as follows:- 1 company in C3, C4S, C4R & C5R: 1 company in C2R in ZOUAVE WOOD: 1 company in R.S3 and 1 company in trenches near YEOMANRY POST: Bn HQ in SANCTUARY WOOD (I24 B.1.8) – Left bivouac at 5.45 pm and reached SANCTUARY WOOD at 8.45 pm: relief completed by 10.35 pm – a quiet night	See map of HOOGE trenches attached: also 8th Bde O.Os Nos 7 & 8
Do	13th Sept.		Our field guns bombarded German trenches north and south of the WALL from 10.30 am to 11.15 am – large parties working on trenches by night.	
Do	14th Sept.		Artillery bombardment by us in forenoon – some retaliation by Germans: large working parties on trenches by night.	

1875 Wt. W593/826 1,000,000 4/15 J.B.C. & A. A.D.S.S./Forms/C. 2118.

1st Bn Gordon Highlanders. 5. September 1915.

WAR DIARY
or
INTELLIGENCE SUMMARY
(Erase heading not required.)

Army Form C. 2118

Instructions regarding War Diaries and Intelligence Summaries are contained in F. S. Regs., Part II. and the Staff Manual respectively. Title Pages will be prepared in manuscript.

Place	Date	Hour	Summary of Events and Information	Remarks and references to Appendices
Bivouac farm H.13.D.5.5.	19th Sept.		Church parade at 6pm – day spent in cleaning clothes and equipment.	
Do.	20th Sept		Usual parades – VLAMERTINGHE was shelled in the evening. The battalion pipers and drummers went to the 2nd Army Grenade School at TURDEGHEM to give an exhibition of piping and dancing: French Officers, who were present, were much impressed by their skill and their display was much appreciated by all –	
Do.	21st Sept.		Usual parades and Training.	
Do.	22nd Sept.		The 3 battalions of the brigade (2nd Royal Scots, 1st Gordon Highrs and 4th Gordon Highrs) not in the trenches were inspected on parade by Lord Kitchener, who, after the inspection, addressed the brigade, remarking on their splendid appearance, thanking them for all the good work they had done in the past and expressing confidence in their carrying out any task entrusted to them in the near future	
Do.	23rd Sept.		Usual parades in morning – Left bivouac at 9pm for HOOGE trenches and relieved 3rd Bn Worcester Regiment, relief completed by 2.15am – usual trench dispositions (as before) taken up.	

1875 Wt. W593/826 1,000,000 4/15 J.B.C. & A. A.D.S.S./Forms/C. 2118.

8.

1st Bn Gordon Highlanders. **WAR DIARY** *or* **INTELLIGENCE SUMMARY** September 1915.

(Erase heading not required.)

Army Form C. 2118

Instructions regarding War Diaries and Intelligence Summaries are contained in F. S. Regs., Part II. and the Staff Manual respectively. Title Pages will be prepared in manuscript.

Place	Date	Hour	Summary of Events and Information	Remarks and references to Appendices
	25th Sept. (contd)		D company (on right) Q47 to Q36 with advanced grenade post at east end of WALL to join up with 4th Gordon Highlanders at Q43, if line Q47 – Q43 was not reached –	
			The following disused communication trenches from our lines to the enemy's were taken as lines of direction and were to be used for communication purposes:- From just north of Q86 to Q40: from Q93 to Q39: from Q95N to Q37: these were all opened up as far as possible during the night and the assaulting parties, preceded by their grenade squads, were enabled to approach along and on either side of them to within a short distance of the German wire before the actual moment of assault – Large ditches running along the north and south sides of the MENIN road were also cleared as much as possible of all debris, etc during the hours of darkness and served the same purpose.	
			The final bombardment commenced at 3·50 am and lifted from the enemy's 1st and 2nd line trenches to his 3rd and 4th lines at 4·5 am, at which hour the leading platoons left our parapet and crawled forward as far as possible: at 4·20 am our guns again lifted to the enemy's trenches further in rear, four mines were exploded near Q12 and Q14 and the assault was delivered all along our line.	
			As stated before, the attack of B and C companies on the left was brought to a standstill as soon as the enemy's wire entanglements were reached and in spite of repeated efforts the attack on this part of the line had to be abandoned as soon as dawn broke: the right company, D, reached the line Q39 – Q36 and joined up with	

1875 Wt. W593/826 1,000,000 4/15 J.B.C. & A. A.D.S.S./Forms/C. 2118.

1st Bn Gordon Highlanders. **WAR DIARY** *or* **INTELLIGENCE SUMMARY** (*Erase heading not required.*) September - 1915. Army Form C. 2118

Instructions regarding War Diaries and Intelligence Summaries are contained in F. S. Regs., Part II. and the Staff Manual respectively. Title Pages will be prepared in manuscript.

Place	Date	Hour	Summary of Events and Information	Remarks and references to Appendices
	25th Sept. (contd)		4th Gordon Highlanders at that point: their casualties were very heavy also and eventually all their grenadiers being killed or wounded and being heavily bombed from the 3 trenches running south from the MENIN ROAD, they had to retire towards Q23 with the 4th Gordon Highlanders and thence to C1 trench: this withdrawal took place about 12 noon, so that shortly after that hour the three attacking companies, or what remained of them, were back in our own trenches.	
			From the commencement of our bombardment the German artillery had directed a heavy and concentrated fire on to the hill of HOOGE and this was maintained throughout the day: as a result the trenches were very badly knocked about and the companies holding them suffered further casualties	
			On our right the battalions succeeded in reaching their objectives, but in each case had to withdraw: on our left the South Lancs. regiment made no progress and the Irish Rifles after gaining a footing in the enemy's lines were forced to retire: the 14th Division were successful in taking BELLEWARDE FARM and surrounding trenches, but they also had to evacuate them during the afternoon with the result that at dusk our line was in its original position.	
			The assault made by the battalion was carried out with the utmost dash and gallantry and had the enemy's wire only been destroyed there is little doubt their objective would have been reached.	
			Many acts of gallantry were performed and will it is hoped receive due recognition:	

1875 Wt W593/826 1,000,000 4/15 J.B.C. & A. A.D.S.S./Forms/C. 2118.

1st Bn. Gordon Highlanders. **WAR DIARY** 10 *or* **INTELLIGENCE SUMMARY** *(Erase heading not required.)* September 1915. Army Form C. 2118

Instructions regarding War Diaries and Intelligence Summaries are contained in F. S. Regs., Part II. and the Staff Manual respectively. Title Pages will be prepared in manuscript.

Place	Date	Hour	Summary of Events and Information	Remarks and references to Appendices
	Sept 25th (contd)		one deed however is especially worthy of record: unfortunately being a grenadier on duty with a company other than his own, his name cannot be traced: on duty with one of the grenade squads attacking with D company, he was one of the first to reach the German trenches: shortly after entering their trenches one leg was blown off above the knee by a shell: he insisted however, although in great pain, in still carrying out his duties at his barricade and, propped up in the firing step, had bags of bombs passed to him, which he hurled at the enemy until he fell back dead—	
			The officers commanding companies were as follows:—	
			A. Coy— Captain M. Dinwiddie. C Coy. Captain G. M. Monteith.	
			B " — Lieut. C. C. Johnstone (Argyll & Sutherland High^rs) D " — 2nd Lt. (temp. Capt.) G. W. Alexander.	
			Captain Alexander was unfortunately wounded during the movement to the assembly positions and the command of D company then devolved on Lieut. C. M. Brown—	
			The casualties of the battalion in this action are shown on attached paper.	

1875 Wt. W593/826 1,000,000 4/15 J.B.C. & A. A.D.S.S./Forms/C. 2118.

Instructions regarding War Diaries and Intelligence Summaries are contained in F. S. Regs., Part II. and the Staff Manual respectively. Title Pages will be prepared in manuscript.

1st Bn Gordon Highlanders.

12

WAR DIARY
or
INTELLIGENCE SUMMARY
(Erase heading not required.)

September 1915

Army Form C. 2118

Place	Date	Hour	Summary of Events and Information	Remarks and references to Appendices
Bivouac farm H.13.D.5.5.	27th Sept. (contd)		consider the attack a failure, it was in reality a victory, as the object of the attack which was to contain the enemy in the YPRES salient, had been gained and that although the fight was far removed from the big effort being made by the French and our 1st Army further south, it was in reality part of the same battle – He concluded his address by remarking that never had any battalion of Gordon Highlanders so worthily upheld the high traditions of that regiment as this battalion had done in the battle of the 25th September –	
Do.	28th Sept.		Usual parades.	
			The battalion was visited in the afternoon by the G.O.C. 3rd Division, Major General A. Haldane, CB. DSO, who thanked the battalion for the excellent work it had done in the recent operations – he recalled the glorious traditions of the regiment and referred with pride to the days he had spent in it: he impressed upon the battalion that although the attack at HOOGE on 25th Sept. might appear to have been a failure, it had really had the effect of drawing German reinforcements of one division and many guns to that sector –	
Trenches I.24 B&D.	29th Sept.		Wet day – The battalion paraded at 5pm and left bivouac for trenches A12, B1 and B2 south of HOOGE, to relieve 7th Bn Border Regt: on arrival at ZILLEBEKE	

1875 Wt. W593/826 1,000,000 4/15 J.B.C. & A. A.D.S.S./Forms/C. 2118.

1st Bn Gordon Highlanders — 13. — September 1915. — Army Form C. 2118

WAR DIARY
or
INTELLIGENCE SUMMARY
(Erase heading not required.)

Instructions regarding War Diaries and Intelligence Summaries are contained in F. S. Regs., Part II. and the Staff Manual respectively. Title Pages will be prepared in manuscript.

Place	Date	Hour	Summary of Events and Information	Remarks and references to Appendices
Trenches 1.24.B+D.	29th Sept (Contd)		however orders were received to remain in the ZILLEBEKE SWITCH trench as probably the relief of the 7th Bn Border Regt. would not take place, owing to the enemy having exploded a mine under B4, attacked the salient there and captured B4 and part of B7: ZOUAVE and SANCTUARY woods and all approaches to the trenches were also being heavily shelled: later on however orders were received to carry out the relief and this was completed by 3.30 am.	
			Owing to the rain the roads were in places nearly knee deep in mud and the battalion experienced a most uncomfortable march and arrived in its new trenches coated in mud and drenched by the heavy rain	
Do.	30th Sept		Quiet morning.	
			A counterattack on the trenches captured by the Germans yesterday was made at 3.15 pm after a short bombardment: the attacking troops consisted of part of the 4th Bn Middlesex Regt, 1 coy Suffolk Regt and 1 company Royal Scots, preceded in each case by bombers: as a result the greater part of the captured trenches were regained, particularly on the left: the battalion had 2 killed and 5 wounded by shell fire.	Vide 8th Bde O.O. No 1 attached.
			A list of officers serving with the battalion during the month is attached, also strength of battalion on this date.	
			[signature] Lt Col. Comdt. 1/Gordon Highrs	

1875 Wt. W593/826 1,000,000 4/15 J.B.C. & A. A.D.S.S./Forms/C. 2118.

DEAD MAN'S BOTTOM
ETANG DE BELLEWARDE
LAKE WOOD
Y WOOD
HOOGE
ZUAVE WOOD
SANCTUARY WOOD
STIRLING CASTLE
MAPLE COPSE
Oxford Street
Grafton St.
G.S. 3 DIV.
SCALE 5,000.
YDS. 200 100 50 0 250 500 750 YDS.
1st Printing Co. R.E., 2nd Army Sec (369).

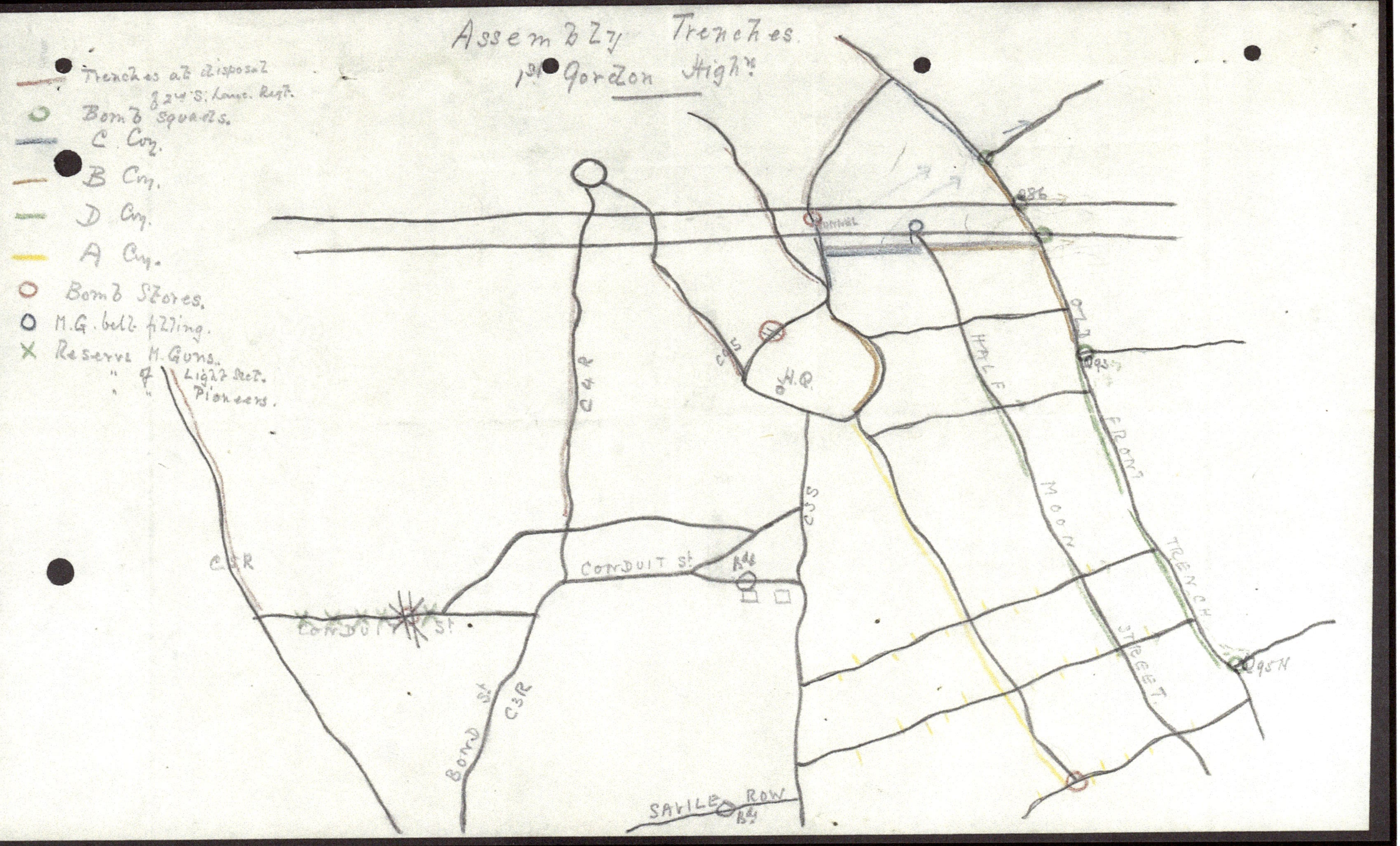

Assembly Trenches.
1st Gordon Highrs.
Trenches at disposal 8 24th S. Lanc. Regt.
Bomb squads.
C Coy.
B Coy.
D Coy.
A Coy.
Bomb Stores.
M.G. belt filling.
Reserve M. Guns.
" " Light Sect.
" " Pioneers.
TUNNEL
H.Q.
C4R
C3S
C5S
C3R
CONDUIT St.
CONDUIT St.
BOND St.
SAVILE ROW
HALF MOON STREET.
FRONT TRENCH.
95N

1st Bn Gordon Highlanders.

Casualties for 25th September 1915.

Company	Killed		Wounded		Wounded & Missing		Missing Believed Killed		Missing		Total	Remarks
	Officers	O.R.	Officers	O.R.	Officers	O.R.	Officers	O.R.	Officers	O.R.		
"A"	1	9	-	50	-	-	-	-	-	2	62	
"B"	1	9	3.	84	-	17	-	-	-	5	119	
"C"	2	9	2.	50	-	1	2	1	-	3.	70	
"D"	2	9	3	48	1	18	-	11	-	-	92	
	6	36	8	232	1	36	2.	12.	-	10	343.	

Marched to trenches. 9.0pm 23-9-15 Strength = Officers 25 Other Ranks 918 Total 943:
25-9-15 Casualties Officers 17. Other Ranks 326 Total. 343:
Returned to Billets 26-9-15. Strength. Officers 8. Other Ranks 592 Total. 600
M.O. & Chaplain 2. Draft 44 Total. 46.
10 636

Instructions regarding War Diaries and Intelligence Summaries are contained in F. S. Regs., Part II. and the Staff Manual respectively. Title Pages will be prepared in manuscript.

1st Gordon Highlanders.

WAR DIARY or INTELLIGENCE SUMMARY

3

(Erase heading not required.)

October 1915.

Army Form C. 2118.

Place	Date	Hour	Summary of Events and Information	Remarks and references to Appendices
Trenches I 24. B & D	11th October		Heavy shelling by Germans between 8 am and 9 am and again in evening – 5 men wounded in R4 (a supporting point in SANCTUARY WOOD). 2 coys of 7th Bn Shropshire Light Infantry arrived at 11 pm for 48 hours instruction in trench duties: both companies, less 1 platoon, went into front trenches to receive instruction from C coy, A coy being withdrawn into reserve dugouts and R4: D company returned to battalion bivouac to absorb its men of new draft.	
Do	12th October		A quiet day – some shelling in evening.	
Do	13th October		Reports received that enemy by bombing had gained a footing in B7 but in the afternoon, when a counterattack had been organised to drive him out, it was found that the trench was not occupied. 2 coys of 7th Bn Shropshire Light Infantry, also Bn H.Q. of that battalion, arrived for instruction in trench duties and relieved their other 2 companies.	
Do	14th October		Thick mist nearly all day – B coy relieved C coy in fire trenches – D coy returned from battalion bivouac, having absorbed new draft – C coy returned to bivouac for same purpose.	
Do	15th October		Thick mist all day – Battalion relieved in trenches by 7th Bn Shropshire Light Infantry and returned to bivouac near VLAMERTINGHE – relief completed by 11.30 pm – Battalion temporarily attached to 76th Inf. Bde.	

1875 Wt. W593/826 1,000,000 4/15 J.B.C. & A. A.D.S.S./Forms/C. 2118.

5

1st Gordon Highlanders

Instructions regarding War Diaries and Intelligence Summaries are contained in F. S. Regs., Part II. and the Staff Manual respectively. Title Pages will be prepared in manuscript.

WAR DIARY
or
INTELLIGENCE SUMMARY
(Erase heading not required.)

October 1915.

Army Form C. 2118.

Place	Date	Hour	Summary of Events and Information	Remarks and references to Appendices
Barns and Dugouts H. 23 B.	21st October		Fine but cold – working parties of 200 men and 100 men employed on same work as on night of 20th Oct – Battalion attached temporarily to 9th Inf Bde	
Do	22nd October		Fine – orders received for battalion to rejoin remainder of 76th Inf Bde in their new billeting area at EECKE: battalion left billets and dugouts at 7.30 pm and marched to square H 11 central (crossing of railway over YPRES – POPERINGHE road just west of YPRES) where 30 busses were waiting to convey battalion to new area: left in busses at 8.10 pm and arrived EECKE at 10pm: battalion billeted in 5 farms – billets comfortable, but companies rather far apart – Rev. I. Logan joined for duty with battalion.	
Billets at EECKE	23rd October		Day spent in cleaning up and settling into billets –	
Do	24th October		Church parade – Major General A. Haldane, CB, DSO, Comdg 3rd Division, presented DCM ribbon to No 3598 Sergt. P. Rennie after church parade –	
Do	25th October		Very wet all day – inspections of kits, etc. Rev. A. Maclean on transfer to GHQ left the battalion to the regret of all ranks –	

1875 Wt. W593/826 1,000,000 4/15 J.B.C. & A. A.D.S.S./Forms/C. 2118.

1st Gordon Highlanders.

Instructions regarding War Diaries and Intelligence Summaries are contained in F. S. Regs., Part II. and the Staff Manual respectively. Title Pages will be prepared in manuscript.

WAR 7 DIARY
or
INTELLIGENCE SUMMARY
(Erase heading not required.)

October 1915.

Army Form C. 2118

Place	Date	Hour	Summary of Events and Information	Remarks and references to Appendices
Billets at EECKE	30th October		Fine - route march - A company taken by Captain Dinwiddie in afternoon to STEENVOORDE to visit 3rd Divisional cinematograph.	
Do.	31st October		Wet day - church parade. Roll of officers and strength of battalion at this date given on attached.	

A W Brown Lt Col.
Comdg 1st Gordon Highrs

1875 Wt. W593/826 1,000,000 4/15 J.B.C. & A. A.D.S.S./Forms/C. 2118.

www.ingramcontent.com/pod-product-compliance
Lightning Source LLC
Chambersburg PA
CBHW081444160426
43193CB00013B/2376